Using Old Testament Hebrew in Preaching

A Guide for
Students and Pastors

PAUL D. WEGNER

Kregel
Academic & Professional

Using Old Testament Hebrew in Preaching: A Guide for Students and Pastors

© 2009 by Paul D. Wegner

Published by Kregel Publications, a division of Kregel, Inc., P.O. Box 2607, Grand Rapids, MI 49501.

Unless otherwise noted, Scripture quotations are the author's translation. Bible permissions can be found on pages 165–66.

The Hebrew font used in this book is New JerusalemU and is available from www.linguistsoftware.com/lgku.htm, +1-425-775-1130.

ISBN 978-0-8254-3936-0

Printed in the United States of America

09 10 11 12 13 / 5 4 3 2 1

*To my Hebrew students at the following schools,
who for over twenty years have
kindly sat under my teaching:*

Trinity International University
Moody Bible Institute
Phoenix Seminary

CONTENTS

PREFACE

*For Ezra had set his heart to study the law of the
Lord and to do [it], and to teach [its] statutes and
judgments in Israel.*

—Ezra 7:10

The faculties of many major seminaries still believe it is crucial for pastors to have a firm grasp of the biblical languages, and I wholeheartedly agree. Students, however, continue to ask me, "Why do I have to learn biblical Hebrew?" Some of the more desperate students add, "I hear that most pastors don't ever use their Greek, let alone their Hebrew, in their preaching after they get out of seminary anyway." Eugene Peterson explains the dilemma of these students well:

> Post-academic life is demanding and decidedly
> unsympathetic to anything that doesn't provide
> quick and obvious returns. We are handed job
> descriptions in which our wonderful languages
> don't even rate a footnote; we acquire families who
> plunge us into urgencies in which Hebrew radicals
> provide no shortcuts; we can't keep up with all the
> stuff thrown at us in easy English—who has time
> for hard Greek? It isn't long before the languages
> are, as we say, "lost."[1]

---

1. Quoted in David W. Baker and Elaine A. Heath, with Morven R. Baker, *More Light on the Path: Daily Scripture Reading in Hebrew and Greek* (Grand Rapids: Baker, 1998), 5.

In the first year of seminary it is easy to think, somewhat naively, "Of course pastors should know Greek and Hebrew and use the original texts every time they preach or teach." However, in time, the initial excitement of learning the biblical languages can get smothered by the amount of Greek and Hebrew vocabulary to memorize and the difficulty of understanding apparently inconsistent grammatical rules. I understand this since I, too, experienced the crushing load of studying Greek and Hebrew as a second-year seminary student. But now that I am "on the other side" and have learned enough Greek and Hebrew to understand why the languages are important, I believe a book like this needs to be written. It seems a terrible waste for students to take one, two, or more years of Greek and/or Hebrew only to enter a busy pastorate and never use the languages. However, it is even worse to hear a pastor butcher a text because no time was dedicated to looking at it in the original language.

This book is written for all Bible school and seminary students who have struggled through at least one year of Hebrew grammar and are wondering how they will ever be able to retain it. It is also written for pastors who need some encouragement to refresh and maintain their knowledge of the biblical languages. I hope this book will help you keep up the good fight and use Hebrew to its fullest. Similar books (e.g., David Alan Black, Gordon D. Fee, Walter L. Liefeld) have been written to help busy pastors use their Greek to prepare sermons, but few resources exist for using Hebrew. I am convinced that modern Christians lack a certain richness and depth in their spiritual lives because they are not hearing the Old Testament preached with the same urgency and power as the New Testament is preached. It is too easy to use the Old Testament merely for illustration without uncovering its true depth.

I agree with David Alan Black who says, "The Word of God must be handled accurately—or not handled at all."[2] My main purpose for this book is to encourage students and pastors to begin using their Hebrew to expound the Old Testament and to bring across the message of a passage both powerfully and accurately. Even though it takes effort and time to understand the grammar and structure of Hebrew

---

2. David Alan Black, *Using New Testament Greek in Ministry: A Practical Guide for Students and Pastors* (Grand Rapids: Baker, 1993), 9.

(e.g., dagheshes, mappiqs, weak verbs), nevertheless the syntax is fairly simple and the time spent trying to understand the meaning of Hebrew texts pays great dividends.

My prayer is that God will use this book to excite you to the fantastic possibility of preaching from the Old Testament with power and accuracy. Lord willing, congregations all over the United States and abroad will be reintroduced to the Old Testament with relevancy and meaning that produces changed lives.

Ezra provides an excellent example of how we should go about our job—to set our hearts to study the law of the Lord so that we can teach it to others (Ezra 7:10). Our job of teaching others God's Word is vital, for the Word "is living and active, sharper than any two-edged sword" (Heb. 4:12). May God give us the ability to handle His Word so well that it does its job not only in our hearts, but also in the hearts of our listeners.

ABBREVIATIONS

AB	Anchor Bible Series. Doubleday
ABD	*Anchor Bible Dictionary.* Edited by David N. Freedman. 6 vols. New York, 1992
BDAG	Bauer, Walter, F. W. Danker, W. F. Arndt, and F. Wilber Gingrich. *A Greek-English Lexicon of the New Testament and Other Early Christian Literature.* 3rd ed. Chicago, 2000
BDB	Brown, F., S. R. Driver, and C. A. Briggs. *Hebrew and English Lexicon of the Old Testament.* Oxford, 1906. Corrected by G. R. Driver, Oxford, 1951. Reprint, Peabody, MA, 1998
BHS	*Biblia Hebraica Stuttgartensia.* Edited by K. Elliger and W. Rudolph. Stuttgart, 1967–77
BSC	Bible Student's Commentary. Zondervan
BST	Bible Speaks Today. InterVarsity
CEV	Contemporary English Version, 1995
DSB	Daily Study Bible. Westminster
EBC	*Expositor's Bible Commentary.* Zondervan
ESV	English Standard Version, 2001
ET	English Text
GKC	*Gesenius' Hebrew Grammar.* Edited by E. Kautzsch. Translated by A. E. Cowley. 2nd ed. Oxford, 1910
GNB	Good News Bible, 1976
GNT	Grundrisse zum Neuen Testament
HALOT	Koehler, L., W. Baumgartner, and J. J. Stamm. *The Hebrew and Aramaic Lexicon of the Old Testament.* Translated and edited under the supervision of M. E. J. Richardson. 5 vols. Leiden, 2000
HER	Hermeneia: A Critical and Historical Commentary on the Bible. Fortress

ICC	International Critical Commentary. Scribner
JBL	*Journal of Biblical Literature*
JPSC	JPS Bible Commentary. Jewish Publication Society of America
JPSTC	JPS Torah Commentary. Jewish Publication Society of America
KJV	King James Version, 1611
LXX	Septuagint
NAC	New American Commentary. Broadman and Holman
NASB	New American Standard Bible, 1977
NASBU	New American Standard Bible, 1995
NBC	New Bible Commentary. Eerdmans
NCB	New Century Bible Commentary. Eerdmans
NEB	New English Bible, 1970
NET	Net Bible, 2005
NIBC	New International Biblical Commentary. Hendrickson
NICOT	New International Commentary on the Old Testament. Eerdmans
NIDOTTE	*The New International Dictionary of Old Testament Theology and Exegesis.* Edited by Willem A. Van Gemeren. 6 vols. Grand Rapids, 1997
NIV	New International Version, 1978
NIVAC	The NIV Application Commentary. Zondervan
NKJV	New King James Version, 1982
NLT	New Living Translation, 1996
NRSV	New Revised Standard Version, 1989
OTL	Old Testament Library. Westminster/John Knox
REB	Revised English Bible, 1989
RSV	Revised Standard Version, 1952
TNIV	Today's New International Version, 2005
TOTC	Tyndale Old Testament Commentaries. Tyndale
TWOT	*Theological Wordbook of the Old Testament.* Edited by R. Laird Harris, Gleason L. Archer Jr., and Bruce K. Waltke. Chicago, 1980
WBC	Word Biblical Commentary. Word
WEC	Wycliffe Exegetical Commentary. Moody

CHAPTER
ONE

THE BIG
QUESTION

HOW WILL KNOWING BIBLICAL HEBREW
HELP ME IN MY MINISTRY?

My only hope for the world is in bringing the
human mind into contact with divine revelation.
—William Gladstone (1809–1898)

If you are a typical Hebrew student, you have spent almost two hundred hours learning vocabulary, about four hundred hours learning the basics of biblical Hebrew grammar, paid several thousand dollars in tuition, and spent about four hundred dollars on books. All this time and expense has been for one basic purpose: to learn to exegete the Hebrew text accurately in order to preach authoritative, relevant sermons to your congregation. Modern Christians have demonstrated a continuing hunger to know God's Word by their attendance at Bible conferences, seminars, studies, and by their purchasing of popular books on the Christian life. However, far too many people avoid the Old Testament. They dare not wander too far into the Old Testament for fear of coming across things they do not understand or, even worse, things that appear to contradict the New Testament.

Epigraph. Cited in Edythe Draper, *Draper's Book of Quotations for the Christian World* (Wheaton, IL: Tyndale, 1992), p. 277, #5094.

Sidney Greidanus succinctly states the problem this way: "It is no secret that the Old Testament is like a lost treasure in the church today."[1] Even well-known accounts from the Old Testament can be confusing:

> An old lady waited on [Joseph] Parker [minister of the City Temple in London] in his vestry after a service to thank him for the help she received from his sermons. "You do throw such wonderful light on the Bible, doctor," she said. "Do you know that until this morning, I had always thought that Sodom and Gomorrah were man and wife?"[2]

There are many good reasons for preaching and teaching from the Old Testament, not the least of which is that it contains at least two-thirds of God's written revelation. But if we are going to teach our congregations more than just the bare minimum, we need the tools to understand the Old Testament ourselves. Whether you are ready to graduate or have been in the pastorate for a number of years, you may wonder how you can find the time to exegete Old Testament passages in the original language with all the other demands of a busy pastorate. You may also find that, even before the degrees are bestowed and the graduation gowns are hung up, the process of forgetting has already begun. Within two years, much of your Hebrew could be lost. On the other hand, all the time and energy you spent learning Hebrew could be just the beginning of a learning process that will provide depth to your knowledge of Scripture and enrich your preaching.

Everyone knows the danger of taking that last Hebrew class (and it is what Hebrew teachers fear most): it could be the last time you crack open your Hebrew Bible. But why is this? Why do so many students forget their Hebrew almost the moment they leave school? And why are there so few books to help students and pastors develop a realistic and practical plan to keep their Hebrew alive and even growing?

1. Sidney Greidanus, *Preaching Christ from the Old Testament: A Contemporary Hermeneutical Method* (Grand Rapids: Eerdmans, 1999), 15.
2. Warren W. Wiersbe and Lloyd M. Perry, *Wycliffe Handbook of Preaching and Preachers* (Chicago: Moody, 1984), 213. See also Arthur Porritt, *The Best I Can Remember* (London: Cassell, 1922), 68.

About halfway through your seminary Hebrew classes, you may have started to wonder if the hard work is worth it. By this point you still have only learned enough grammar and vocabulary to translate very rudimentary Hebrew sentences. And then you hear how hard it is to learn those dreaded weak verbs.

It is not an unrealistic goal to be able to maintain your Hebrew after graduation. In fact, you may even have some fun along the way. For instance, using the original language during devotions will not only feed your soul, but it may also uncover gems for future messages. However, it is important to set realistic goals and devise a plan to retain your Hebrew. I have often said that I would rather students get Bs in Hebrew with the intention of using the language for the rest of their lives than to get As but be so exhausted by the end of their coursework that they never want to see a Hebrew text again.

WHY STUDY HEBREW ANYWAY?

I, like every other teacher of biblical languages, have been asked hundreds of times if studying Hebrew is necessary. Often the question sounds like this: "Aren't the English translations of the Bible accurate enough and won't they be sufficient for me to teach from? Why should I make another translation? I will never be able to make as good a translation as those Hebrew experts, anyway." Most modern Bible translations are indeed accurate and provide a suitable guideline for teaching. However, Dennis Magary notes:

> As fine as our contemporary translations are, as carefully as they have been prepared, a translation is still a translation. It is and will always be at least one step removed from the original. An English version, a translation of the Hebrew text in any language, is an interpretation, a commentary reflecting critical and interpretive decisions by a host of scholars. Translators have made numerous decisions regarding the meaning of words, the syntax of clauses, [and] the referent of a pronoun.[3]

---

3. Dennis R. Magary, "Keeping Your Hebrew Healthy," in *Preaching the Old Testament*, ed. Scott M. Gibson (Grand Rapids: Baker, 2006), 30.

Translations are sufficient to meet the needs of most people. But for a pastor or teacher of God's Word, they are only the beginning of serious study. The person who is willing to delve into the original languages will be rewarded with depths of meaning to which the average person reading the Bible does not have access. Even just a few examples will highlight the importance of reading an Old Testament passage in the original Hebrew.

Genesis 1:2 says that the earth was "formless and void" (תֹהוּ וָבֹהוּ *tōhû wābōhû*), but what does that mean? The text goes on to explain that in the first three days God shaped the earth to correct its formlessness. God used the second set of three days to fill the earth, addressing its emptiness or void. After day six the earth was no longer "formless and void" and God called it "very good." It is interesting that the only other place where the phrase "formless and void" (תֹהוּ וָבֹהוּ *tōhû wābōhû*) is used is Jeremiah 4:23 where it refers to the destruction by the Babylonians in 586 B.C. This suggests that Israel's sins had returned the earth to its pre-creation chaotic state. It is easy to miss these connections in English translations.

Another good example is found in the first part of Psalm 2:12, a very difficult verse to interpret. Most English translations render the underlying text as "kiss the Son," a very literal translation in which *son* is a translation of the Aramaic word בַּר (*bar*, "son"); rather than the Hebrew word בֵּן (*bēn*, "son"), which occurs in verse 7. Noting this subtle shift to Aramaic helps the preacher understand the intended audience of the psalm. By shifting to Aramaic in verse 12, the author of Psalm 2 subtly reminds the readers of the Gentile nations who would have been familiar with the Aramaic trade language, but possibly ignorant of Hebrew. The typical English reader would not even be aware of the change in language.

In addition, members of your congregation will often have questions about differences between modern translations. Congregants may ask which translation is correct, or which translation is better and why. You, as the professional, will need to be able to answer these questions, and you will need to examine the Hebrew or Greek text to know which translation is more accurate. At that point you will have an excellent opportunity to teach members about a new level of Bible study. Or, you will lose this opportunity and will need to direct the would-be learner to someone else for the answers. In one sense, modern translations are like training wheels—they can provide balance and guidance to someone new to translation. But to get serious about riding a bicycle, the training wheels have to come off eventually. You may not be able to make as good a translation as "those Hebrew experts," but every translation has to make compromises. Creating your own translation will allow you to discover the crucial issues involved in translating specific passages and to make some decisions for yourself concerning them.

If you are (or will be) a preaching pastor with regular opportunity to open God's Word to your congregation, then you must be better prepared and trained than those in your congregation. You may have doctors, lawyers, dentists, business people, or other trained professionals in your congregation. They have each studied hard to do well in their professions and they will expect no less from you. Any professional should be better prepared than their clients. I don't need to know much about how my car works to drive it, but my mechanic needs the knowledge and expertise to fix it. In a similar way, a pastor needs to work with the original languages to answer certain questions and to speak accurately on certain issues. How will you be able to correct someone's erroneous thinking if you cannot be sure what the Greek or Hebrew text says? How will you know if commentaries or Bible study tools are correct? The members of your congregation will want to know what *you* think since they know and trust you; they have never heard of F. F. Bruce or D. A. Carson. These scholars can be your guides, but you will need to guide those in your congregation.

Sometimes students say, "I've already learned Greek, so how important is it for me to learn Hebrew too?" This question always strikes me as odd. I would hope knowledge of Greek would impact our understanding of the New Testament and that this would extend to our preaching and teaching. So wouldn't learning Hebrew be just as valuable for understanding the Old Testament? It is like asking which is more important to learn: how to put together a wedding ceremony or how to conduct a funeral? Both ceremonies are important at different times in people's lives—both are necessary. In a similar way, learning both Greek and Hebrew provides the foundation for helping other people understand the full counsel of God.

Paul writes to Timothy and assures him that "All Scripture is God breathed and useful for teaching, for reproof, for correction, for training in righteousness; so that the person of God may be fully equipped for every good work" (2 Tim. 3:16–17). At the point in history in which he wrote, Paul was primarily speaking about the Old Testament. In past generations it was not unusual to be well trained in both Greek and Hebrew:

> Jonathan Edwards, educated at home under his father's care, had thorough knowledge of Greek, Hebrew, and Latin when he entered Yale before the age of 13 in 1716. Likewise, J. A. Alexander (1838–1860) one of the second generation professors of theology at Princeton Theological Seminary, knew the rudiments of Greek, Hebrew, and Latin by his tenth birthday. The founder of Southern Seminary, James Pedigru Boice learned Greek from a Sunday School teacher.[4]

If the original languages are so important for understanding and exegeting Scripture, why have many seminaries and Bible schools dropped the original languages from their curricula?[5] Why aren't students demanding to be taught the original languages? To neglect the study of the biblical languages is to set our sights far too low. Some pastors today would have a difficult time finding the book of Habakkuk, let alone explaining what it means or why it is important. If pastors cannot perform these functions, imagine how difficult they are for laypeople. So the question remains, how can we retain Greek and Hebrew amid the demands of a busy pastorate?

PLANNING FOR SUCCESS

Before you throw in the towel and sell all those expensive Hebrew books to some unsuspecting beginning student, let's consider where you are and what you have gained in

---

4. Gregg Strawbridge, "Thoughts on the Importance of Greek in Education and Training," http://www.wordmp3.com/gs/greekimportance.htm (accessed March 25, 2006).
5. H. Richard Niebuhr, Daniel D. Williams, and James M. Gustafson, *The Advancement of Theological Education* (New York: Harper, 1957), 92–93.

the process of Hebrew study. You began this study because you felt that undertaking it was the only way to know adequately what the biblical texts are saying (and that is still true). You believed you had the perseverance and patience to learn another language (or two) and you have either accomplished this goal or are moving closer to it. So what you really need now is a plan to use your learning to exegete properly and prepare sermons. This book is intended to provide the plan or method for you not only to keep using your Hebrew, but to help you become more and more proficient in your use of it.

This book is organized as follows: Chapter 2 helps you determine the best Hebrew tools and discusses how to use them. Chapter 3 provides an overview of the exegetical process to help you determine the meaning of a Hebrew text. Chapter 4 describes the process of moving from exegesis to sermon. Finally, chapter 5 discusses how to make the best use of your time when studying the Hebrew text, as well as offering several practical ways to use your Hebrew. The book provides a plan that can be adjusted to your own schedule and the unique needs of your congregation. It is intended to help you become more efficient in your study time. Wherever possible, I will describe the most useful tools or guidelines and share how I personally allocate my time.

So how do you get started? First, let's look at your motivations and objectives in acquiring Hebrew. Then we will consider the methods that will be the most advantageous for you.

Your Motives: Why Did You Learn Hebrew?

Shepherding God's flock is a high calling (see 1 Tim. 3:1) and comes with great responsibilities. Paul encourages Timothy to "hold fast to the standard of sound words" which he had heard from Paul. Timothy was to "guard through the Holy Spirit" the "good thing" with which he had been entrusted (2 Tim. 1:13–14).

In the next chapter, Paul writes, "The things which you have heard from me through many witnesses, entrust these to faithful people who will be able to teach others also" (2 Tim. 2:2). James offers a similar exhortation and warns, "Let not many of you become teachers, my brothers, knowing that we will receive a stricter judgment" (James 3:1). If we have accepted the call to become teachers of God's Word, then we also need to realize the awesome responsibility we carry and train to do the job to the best of our abilities. This endeavor will pay rich dividends, but it will come at a cost.

Your Objectives: How Fluent Would You Like to Be in Hebrew?

This decision will depend upon many things: (1) how much time and how many resources you have, (2) what goals you have for preaching (do you preach regularly or only occasionally?), and (3) what level of expertise you would like to obtain. While these criteria may help determine what level of proficiency to work toward, don't sell yourself short—these decisions will affect the rest of your life. Aim high, and at the same time be realistic. You can, of course, do further study if circumstances change, but it gets harder to pursue education as you become older. Family commitments, financial constraints, and health issues often accompany the years. David Alan Black recommends following the guidelines used by the Foreign Service Institute of the United States Department of State and the Educational Testing Service to determine your optimal level of proficiency.[6] They are the four R-levels (i.e., "reading levels") for language:

R-1 (Elementary Proficiency)

In a spoken language, those at the R-1 level of learning know basic phrases and can formulate rudimentary sentences, but easily get lost in conversation with a native speaker who speaks fast or uses more complicated words. In a written language a person can work out rudimentary or simplified sentences such as those used in Hebrew grammars. Such a person may be able to read some of the easier parts of the Hebrew Bible but still depends heavily on Hebrew dictionaries and commentaries. Those at this stage probably also need to follow a literal English translation of the Hebrew text. At this elementary level of proficiency, a person could begin to rate the quality of a commentary. If this is the level of proficiency you would like to attain, then invest in quality Hebrew grammatical aids. This would include a good Hebrew grammar; a Hebrew lexicon (dictionary); a parsing guide (lists specific verb forms and their parsings—stem

---

6. David Alan Black, *Using New Testament Greek in Ministry: A Practical Guide for Students and Pastors* (Grand Rapids: Baker, 1993), 27–28.

[*binyan*], tense, person, gender, number, root, and meaning); basic syntax books; and quality commentaries. A good computer program (e.g., Logos, BibleWorks, Accordance) would be one of your best investments at this level. Spend your time learning basic Hebrew vocabulary (about one hundred thirty of the most frequent words, approximately 68 percent of the Old Testament Hebrew vocabulary) and the basic keys for determining verb forms and the nuances of the various verbs stems (*binyanim*).

R-2 (Limited Working Proficiency)

Those at the R-2 proficiency level can read some of the easier parts of the Hebrew Bible but still need to consult a lexicon regularly for vocabulary. They are able to parse many of the Hebrew strong verb forms and some of the easier weak verb forms. If this is the level of proficiency you would like to attain, you will need a working vocabulary of about three hundred of the most frequent Hebrew words (about 78 percent of the Hebrew vocabulary of the Old Testament), familiarity with the keys for recognizing verb forms, to read more advanced Hebrew grammars, and to spend about one-half hour each day translating from the Hebrew Bible (at least initially—later this could decrease). If you use a computer program, try to parse the verb forms first and then check them. Try to work out the structure and meaning of the passage and then compare various English translations to your own.

R-3 (Professional Proficiency)

Those at the R-3 level of proficiency can read from most of the Hebrew Bible but still need to consult a lexicon regularly for vocabulary. They are able to parse many of the Hebrew verb forms, both strong and weak, though they may need to look up some of the more difficult forms. If you would like this level of proficiency, then you will need a working vocabulary of about six hundred fifty of the most frequent Hebrew words (over 86 percent of the Old Testament Hebrew vocabulary), proficient knowledge of the keys for recognizing the strong and weak verb forms, to read more advanced Hebrew grammars, and to spend about one hour a day translating the Hebrew Bible (at least initially—later this could decrease). With practice, you will be able to translate fairly quickly with a computer program, though you may still struggle over some of the more difficult verb forms and sentence structures. It will be helpful at this point to read the full entries for words in the Hebrew lexicons to make sure you understand the full range of meaning. You should frequently check Hebrew grammars and syntax books to understand the meaning of the passage and be able to outline the grammar of Hebrew sentences.

R-4 (Full Proficiency)

Those at the R-4 level of proficiency can read from any part of the Hebrew Bible, but still need to consult a lexicon regularly for certain vocabulary (even at this level, since there are almost eight thousand five hundred vocabulary words, more than sixteen hundred of which are *hapax legomena* [i.e., words that occur only once]). Such learners of Hebrew can parse almost all of the Hebrew verb forms, both strong and weak, though it may still be necessary to look up the most difficult forms. If you would like to obtain this level of proficiency, you will need a working vocabulary of about fifteen hundred words (about 93 percent of the Old Testament Hebrew vocabulary), proficiency in recognizing the strong and weak verb forms, to read more advanced Hebrew grammars, and to spend two hours daily translating from the Hebrew Bible (at least initially—later this could decrease). With practice, you will be able to translate very quickly with a computer program since you already know many of the words, but you may still struggle over some of the most difficult verb forms and some of the Hebrew syntax.

By setting realistic expectations you will be able to plan ahead and work to acquire the necessary skills. Knowing what you are aiming for will help you avoid discouragement and give you a better chance of reaching your goals. An R-1 level proficiency could be achieved with a one-semester course dedicated to providing basic Hebrew grammar and tools. You could advance to an R-2 level of proficiency with a full year of grammar study. The remaining levels take significantly longer to reach. With this in mind, it is better to think of learning Hebrew as a marathon and not a sprint. Some schools offer condensed courses of Hebrew in summer school, but a longer, more steady progression toward the goal will probably suit most people's learning needs much better. Once you reach the R-2 proficiency level, you can build to the higher levels through self-study.

Your Methods: What Is the Best Way for You to Learn Hebrew?

All students learn differently. They pursue different goals and varying levels of skill. No single Hebrew course can meet everyone's needs, so each person will have to supplement instruction to some degree. As noted above, there are three crucial elements for learning Hebrew: (1) vocabulary, (2) basic grammar, and (3) practice in translating the original text. Any plan for learning Hebrew must include at least these basic elements. Everyone experiences growth spurts in learning Hebrew, but the key to long-term success in language acquisition is steady, prolonged growth. Simply put, a meager goal of two or three verses a day over time is better than trying to attack large chunks of text and burning out.

Learn How the Language Works

Learning any language becomes drudgery when the instructor emphasizes *quantity* over *understanding*. Teachers guilty of this method may themselves have had ineffective instruction; or perhaps insufficient proficiency limits their ability to explain the language's intricacies. During my first two years of teaching Hebrew, I frequently went to a more experienced colleague to ask questions about how the language worked. It was the best learning experience I could ever have had. It is a running joke in most Hebrew classes that Hebrew is a very consistent language except in all the places where it is inconsistent. However, English can be equally challenging to learn:

> English is a crazy language. There is no egg in eggplant, nor ham in hamburger; neither apple nor pine in pineapple. English muffins weren't invented in England or French fries in France. Sweetmeats are candies while sweetbreads, which aren't sweet, are meat. We take English for granted. But if we explore its paradoxes, we find that quicksand can work slowly, boxing rings are square and a guinea pig is neither from Guinea nor is it a pig. . . .
>
> English was invented by people, not computers, and it reflects the creativity of the human race (which, of course, isn't a race at all). That is

why, when the stars are out, they are visible, but when the lights are out, they are invisible.[7]

If you are still in a position to choose, I challenge you to study under the best teachers—those who really understand the language and not those who just let you slide through with an A. Ask the tough questions like, "Why does the language work this way?" and "How will this knowledge help me feed my future congregation?" If you do not understand aspects of Hebrew, ask to have "language labs" with your professor. Use this extra time to carefully go over what you are missing or do not understand.[8]

Learning Hebrew is not easy, but be willing to push yourself. We live in a culture that readily accepts mediocrity and relativism. If truth is relative, then there would be little point in working hard to determine what the Bible says, much less compounding our frustration by learning Hebrew. But truth is not relative and the Bible helps us to know what really is true. This generation of pastors needs to be better prepared than any previous one so that people can know the truth by which God illumines us.

To pursue this role, you should take adequate time to learn the biblical languages. While in school, it would be helpful to arrange your schedule so that you do not have your hardest classes in a semester when you are taking Hebrew or Greek. If this means extending your seminary training, then by all means do it. Speed is not as important as being prepared.

Make It Practical

In 1981, Walter Kaiser pointed out a significant deficiency in seminary education:

> I have been aware for some time now of a gap that has existed in academic preparation for the ministry. It is the gap that exists between the study of

7. Richard Lederer, "English Is a Crazy Language: An Excerpt from the Introduction," http://web.mit.edu/wchuang/www/humor/college/English_is_Crazy.html (accessed May 18, 2006).
8. For a helpful book on understanding the workings of biblical languages, see Peter James Silzer and Thomas John Finley, *How Biblical Languages Work: A Student's Guide to Learning Greek and Hebrew* (Grand Rapids: Kregel, 2004).

the biblical text (most frequently in the original languages of Hebrew, Aramaic, and Greek) and the actual delivery of messages to God's people. Very few centers of biblical and homiletical training have ever taken the time or effort to show the student how one moves from analyzing the text over to constructing a sermon that accurately reflects that same analysis and is directly dependent upon it.[9]

George Müller, after having read the Bible through one hundred times with increasing delight, made this statement: "I look upon it as a lost day when I have not had a good time over the Word of God. Friends often say, 'I have so much to do, so many people to see, I cannot find time for Scripture study.' Perhaps there are not many who have more to do than I. For more than half a century I have never known one day when I had not more business than I could get through. For 4 years I have had annually about 30,000 letters, and most of these have passed through my own hands.

"Then, as pastor of a church with 1,200 believers, great has been my care. Besides, I have had charge of five immense orphanages; also, at my publishing depot, the printing and circulating of millions of tracts, books, and Bibles; but I have always made it a rule never to begin work until I have had a good season with God and His Word. The blessing I have received has been wonderful."[10]

---

9. Walter C. Kaiser, *Toward an Exegetical Theology: Biblical Exegesis for Preaching and Teaching* (Grand Rapids: Baker, 1981), 8.
10. Sermon Illustrations, http://www.Sermonillustrations.com/a-z/b/bible_study_of.htm (accessed August 22, 2006).

Kaiser then goes on to describe the critical gap "between the steps generally outlined in most seminary or biblical training classes in exegesis and the hard realities most pastors face every week as they prepare their sermons."[11] There is a big difference between an Old Testament research paper and an Old Testament sermon. Since the time Dr. Kaiser wrote these words, several books have appeared to address this issue. Unfortunately, two questions continue to slip through the cracks: (1) Why should pastors use Hebrew to develop their sermons? and (2) What is a reasonable method for busy pastors to use to prepare their sermons from the original languages? We have already addressed the first question, and we will address the second later in this book.

There is one additional area that is often overlooked in lessons on grammar and homiletics. After parsing, translating, and digging for the meaning of a passage, you are ready to reflect upon how it can feed your soul. How do you apply the new truths that you have learned? For example, what does it mean in Psalm 23:3 that "He restores my soul"? How does this work? The Hebrew root שׁוּב (šûb "to return") apparently speaks in this context of a person's return to a state of quietness after a period of turmoil. In other words, God is the one who can restore quietness and peace to our inner beings after a time of great upheaval or turmoil. He is the calm after the storm. Other psalms refer to God as a "rock" or "shelter" in the midst of the storm, which suggests that he is our protection when things around us are treacherous. Psalm 23 goes on to say that "He leads me in paths of righteousness for his name's sake." The word *paths* brings to mind the constant weight of a wagon going over the same roads time and time again so that a path is worn in the ground. God leads us in the firm and straight paths of righteousness for the sake of his name. Since God's honor is at stake, He will always lead us in those well-worn paths of truth because that is his character. He wants us to reflect his character.

The Hebrew Bible can be a source of spiritual renewal and it is important to see it in this light. As you learn new Hebrew words or translate new passages, think about their ramifications for your spiritual growth. This is one of the primary ways you can use Hebrew to feed yourself and your congregation. As the Word of God feeds you through your

11. Kaiser, *Toward an Exegetical Theology*, 18.

study of the Hebrew text, use those insights to reach new depths in your preaching.

CONCLUSION

The goal of this chapter is to help you develop and maintain excitement about using biblical Hebrew to unlock and delve into the richness of the Old Testament. Martin Luther urged us to "zealously hold to the [biblical] languages," because they are "the sheath in which this sword of the Spirit is contained."[12] Learning Hebrew need not be a sterile experience of only memorizing vocabulary words and verb forms. Instead it can be a means for you to nourish your spiritual life and share the insights with others.

THINGS TO CONSIDER

Be sure to think through the following questions about your ministry before you go to the next chapter:

1. Do I have a strong desire to expound God's Word in order to lead people into a deeper understanding of Scripture?

2. What level of fluency in biblical Hebrew do I want to work toward?

3. Do I have the time, energy, and resources to learn biblical Hebrew at that level?

4. Am I willing to use the Hebrew Bible to help nourish my own spiritual life? If you answered no to this question, then prayerfully consider what better way there could be to understand the Old Testament than to read God's Word in the original languages. Is there any better gift that you could give to your congregation?

FURTHER READING

Carson, D. A. *For the Love of God: A Daily Companion for Discovering the Riches of God's Word*. Wheaton, IL: Crossway, 2006.

---

12. "To the Councilmen of All Cities in Germany That They Establish and Maintain Christian Schools," in *Luther's Works*, ed. Jaroslav Pelikan and Helmut T. Lehmann (Philadelphia: Muhlenberg, 1962), 45:359–60.

Craddock, Fred B. *Preaching.* Nashville: Abingdon, 1985. See especially pages 13–65.

Gibson, Scott M. "Challenges to Preaching the Old Testament." In *Preaching the Old Testament,* edited by Scott M. Gibson, 21–27. Grand Rapids: Baker, 2006.

Kaiser, Walter C. *Towards an Exegetical Theology: Biblical Exegesis for Preaching and Teaching.* Grand Rapids: Baker, 1981.

Magary, Dennis R. "Keeping Your Hebrew Healthy." In *Preaching the Old Testament,* edited by Scott M. Gibson, 29–55. Grand Rapids: Baker, 2006.

Piper, John. *Brothers, We Are Not Professionals: A Plea to Pastors for Radical Ministry.* Nashville: Broadman & Holman, 2002. See especially pages 81–88.

Spurgeon, Charles H. *Lectures to My Students.* Grand Rapids: Zondervan, 1954. See especially pages 7–52.

CHAPTER
TWO

TOOLS
OF THE TRADE

WHAT ARE THE CRUCIAL TOOLS THAT I SHOULD GET?

*It depends on what we read, after all manner of
Professors have done their best for us. The true
University of these days is a Collection of Books.*
—Thomas Carlyle

I will always remember Mrs. Rasmussen, my second grade
teacher, who constantly reminded us that we needed to
bring the tools of our trade to school. The same goes for
preachers. In fact, having the right tools will make the difference between an average pastor and a great pastor. Just like
a mechanic needs the right tools to fix a car or a carpenter
needs the right tools to build a shelf, so also you need the
right tools to understand the biblical text and present it
properly. The late Dr. Donald Grey Barnhouse, pastor of
the Tenth Presbyterian Church in Philadelphia, said, "If I
had only three years to serve the Lord, I would spend two
of them studying and preparing."[1] The job of determining

Epigraph. Quoted in Thomas Carlyle, *On Heros, Hero-Worship, and
the Heroic in History: Six Lectures.* Reported, with Emendations and
Additions (London: James Fraser, 1841), 262.
1. Dr. Charles R. Swindoll, excerpted from the inaugural address at
Dallas Theological Seminary, October 27, 1994, and quoted in *Presidential
Inauguration*, a special edition of *DTS News*, December 1994, 2.

the meaning of an Old Testament text demands precision, which requires the wisdom of scholars and teachers. Some tools are critical to the task; others will help save time and effort.

THE PURPOSE OF THIS CHAPTER

Pastors must continually read to stay abreast of both current events and critical biblical scholarship in order to help their congregations understand the relevance of the biblical texts. This chapter will guide you as you choose the books that are most essential for in-depth study of biblical Hebrew passages. Douglas Stuart reminds all would-be exegetes that "without the proper tools, an exegesis can't go very far."[2] I have annotated the following collection of important exegetical tools to help you understand their purpose and importance. My goal is to help you build your library wisely. Books are expensive, so I will limit my suggestions to the tools most needed in each step of the exegetical process. You may only need to purchase some of these works once in a lifetime unless a helpful update or an expanded new edition becomes available.

UNDERSTANDING RESEARCH BOOKS

Listed below is a selection of a wide range of quality tools to help pastors effectively teach the Old Testament. I have included three kinds of resources: first, resources for maintaining Hebrew language skills; second, materials for understanding the Old Testament world and particular books; and third, computer resources for everything from biblical Hebrew to sermon illustrations. Since readers will be at different levels in their knowledge of Hebrew, some may need tools to brush up on the rudiments of Hebrew; others may not need such basics. Choose the resources that will help you where you are weak. The following general guidelines can help you select the right type of books for your library.

First, some tools that may have been considered "cheater's tools" or "crib tools" when used in Hebrew class are useful time savers when trying to keep your Hebrew alive. David Alan Black insists that ministers "should never

---

2. Douglas Stuart, *Old Testament Exegesis: A Handbook for Students and Pastors*, 3rd ed. (Louisville: Westminster John Knox, 2001), 3.

hesitate to use any 'crib' necessary to get into the languages. The dictum here is, 'Halitosis is better than no breath at all,' as one preacher has put it. Interlinears, parsing guides, analytical lexicons, or any other aid can, and should be used without guilt or apology."[3] Second, be aware that most Hebrew scholars consider some so-called helps useless or even detrimental. Rather than naming any of these, I will list only the tools that are of sufficient quality for good research.

Finally, as important as these tools are, the biblical text itself is more important than tools could ever be. Tools can never be a reasonable substitute for the Bible. Psalm 19:8–9 (English vv. 7–8) reminds us how important God's Word is:

> The law of the LORD is complete, restoring the soul;
> The testimony of the LORD is faithful, making wise the simple.
> The precepts of the LORD are upright, rejoicing the heart;
> The commandment of the LORD is pure, enlightening the eyes.

George Müller makes the following observation regarding the study of Scripture itself:

> I had been a student of divinity in the university [sic] of Halle, and had written many a long manuscript at the lectures of the professors of divinity; but I had not come to this blessed Book in the right spirit. At length I came to it as I had never done before. I said, "The Holy Ghost is the Teacher now in the Church of Christ; the Holy Scriptures are now the rule given by God; from them I must learn His mind,—I will now prove it." I locked my door. I put my Bible on the chair. I fell down before the chair, and spent three hours prayerfully reading the word of God; and I unhesitatingly say that in those three hours I learned more than in

---

3. David Alan Black, *Using New Testament Greek in Ministry. A Practical Guide for Students and Pastors* (Grand Rapids: Baker, 1993), 35.

any previous three, six, or twelve months' period of my life.[4]

> B orn to be battered . . . the loving phone book. Underline it, circle things, write in the margins, turn down page corners, the more you use it, the more valuable it gets to be. [Even more true for Scriptures.][5]

Reading the biblical text is important, and reading it with understanding is even more so. Tools are only valuable when they help us better understand the depth and richness of God's Word.

PART I: FOURTEEN ESSENTIAL RESOURCES

The following works represent fourteen foundational tools to have in your library for Old Testament study. In each category, I have listed first the most important resource (each marked with a star)—others can be gradually added over time, if necessary. For about $750 ($400 if bought used) you can have the essential tools for quality Hebrew exegesis. It is wise at this point to decide whether investing in a computer program would better meet your needs than buying these books in print. I recommend that a busy pastor or student buy a good computer program and learn to use it well. It will save a great deal of time and provide you with the incentive to continue study in the original languages. Some computer programs contain many or all of the following works and are able to retrieve information quickly, but they are not for everyone.

One word of caution, if you are not willing to invest the time it takes to learn how to use these wonderful programs, they will sit idly on your computers. You know what type of person you are. Would you rather hold a book than

---

4. George Müller, *A Narrative of Some of the Lord's Dealings with George Müller*, 2 vols. (Muskegon, MI: Dust & Ashes Publications, 2003), 2:741.
5. Ad in South Central Bell Telephone Company Yellow Pages. "Sermon Illustrations," http://www.sermonillustrations.com/a-z/b/bible_study_of.htm (accessed August 22, 2006).

read it on-screen or print it out yourself? If you are not reasonably comfortable with computers but would like to buy one of these programs, you may need to ask a friend or someone in your church to help you learn how to use them. This would be a beautiful way for technologically savvy people to use their gifts to build up God's kingdom. Why not have a "computer geek" teach a Sunday school class on "Computers and Bible Study" or "Computer Bible Studies for Dummies"?

If you decide to go the computer route, then I suggest buying a laptop computer. It costs more, but the portability of a laptop allows you to bring your library with you. If someone asks you a question, then you have the information at your fingertips to give an informed answer.

1. An English Translation

While an English Bible is the object of our study, it is also a tool for unlocking the original language of the biblical text. English translations are usually developed by a committee of Hebrew and Greek experts who have carefully worked through the biblical texts to provide an accurate translation. English translations can serve as a guide or standard for your translations of the texts.

Choosing a Bible translation can be difficult. It is wise to preach out of the translation most of the people in your congregation use, or to decide as a congregation on a recommended version. This will largely depend upon the type of congregation you have and the intended use of the translation. The following guidelines may prove helpful:

A. There is no perfect translation; each has strengths and weaknesses. Balancing these strengths against the weaknesses should guide the choice of a translation for your church.

B. Certain translation principles and techniques form the foundation for each translation. Some translations are intended to be word-for-word (e.g., NASBU, RSV, ESV); some are more paraphrastic in nature (e.g., NLT, GNB, MSG); and others provide a dynamic equivalence, which attempts to make the same impact upon modern readers as the text did in biblical times (e.g., NIV, TNIV).

C. Some translations may be more appropriate for certain situations and audiences. Older congregations may prefer more traditional translations (KJV, NKJV, RSV, NRSV, NASBU, etc.), while younger congregations may prefer more contemporary translations (NLT, NIV, ESV, etc.). Churches that concentrate on Bible exposition will probably prefer a more literal translation, and seeker-sensitive churches may choose a Bible that is more user-friendly to contemporary audiences (MSG, GNB, etc.).

D. I would avoid certain translations because of the theological decisions underlying them (NEB, REB). In 2 Timothy 3:16, the NEB reads, "Every inspired scripture has its use" (and the REB, similarly, reads, "All inspired scripture has its use") instead of "All Scripture is inspired and useful," the first implying there may be some Scripture that is not inspired. Other translations have made questionable textual critical decisions. For example, at the end of 1 Samuel 10 the NRSV translators inserted an addition to the text supported only by a Qumran document [4QSam^a] and Josephus [*Antiquities* 6:68–71]). By and large, however, most modern translations are accurate and reliable.

E. Most modern translations also have a study Bible format. A study Bible contains notes on difficult passages at the bottom of the page and can be a good place to start even if you may not always agree with the interpretations in the notes. Study Bibles often have useful tools like cross-references, maps, and concordances. These notes and tools can be handy when a church member asks for the reference of a specific verse or has questions about a particular passage.

Pastors should choose a literal translation for Bible study (e.g., NASBU, RSV, ESV), especially as a guide when translating the Hebrew text. It is also useful to compare and contrast translations to bring out various nuances of a word or to identify a textual issue for further examination. There are two easy ways to compare translations: use either a computer program or use a book such as *The Bible from Twenty-six Translations*.[6] The following chart provides a quick overview of the most popular English translations (a more in-depth summary of translations can be found in Paul D. Wegner, *The Journey from Texts to Translations*).[7]

NAME	DATE	TRANSLATION TYPE	PURPOSE
New American Standard Bible (NASB/NASBU)	1977; Updated 1995	Literal, word-for-word	Good for Bible study and teaching
Revised Standard Version (RSV)	1952	Literal, word-for-word	Good for Bible study and teaching
English Standard Version (ESV)	2001	Literal, word-for-word	Good for Bible study and teaching
New Revised Standard Version (NRSV)	1989	Literal, word-for-word	Good for Bible study, but not as accurate for textual criticism
New King James Version (NKJV)	1982	Literal, word-for-word	Good for Bible study, but does not use the best text in the NT
Holman Christian Standard Bible (HCSB)	2004	Optimal equivalence (mixture of literal and dynamic equivalence)	Good for Bible study and reading
New International Version (NIV)	1978	Dynamic equivalence	Good for reading and understanding; sometimes lacks precision.
Today's New International Version (TNIV)	2006	Dynamic equivalence	Good for reading and understanding; sometimes lacks precision
New Living Translation (NLT)	1996	Dynamic equivalence	Good for reading and understanding
Contemporary English Version (CEV)	2000	Paraphrastic	Good for understanding
Good News Bible (GNB)	1976	Paraphrastic	Good for understanding, especially for children or for those with English as a second language
The Message (MSG)	1993-2002	Very paraphrastic	Good for understanding, but sometimes compromises accuracy

6. Curtis Vaughan, ed., *The Word: The Bible from Twenty-six Translations* (Gulfport, MS: Mathis, 1991).

7. Paul D. Wegner, *The Journey from Texts to Translations* (Grand Rapids: Baker, 1999).

Examining multiple translations prepares you for translational or text critical difficulties. For example, see the variety of translations for 1 Samuel 13:1:

> NKJV: "Saul reigned one year, and when he had reigned two years over Israel . . ."

> NASB (1977): "Saul was *forty* years old when he began to reign, and he reigned *thirty*-two years over Israel."

> NASBU (1995): "Saul was *thirty* years old when he began to reign, and he reigned *forty*-two years over Israel."

> NIV: "Saul was *thirty* years old when he became king, and he reigned over Israel *forty*-two years."

> RSV: "Saul was . . . years old when he began to reign; and he reigned . . . and two years over Israel."

> ESV: "Saul was . . . years old when he began to reign, and he reigned . . . and two years over Israel."

Generally there is not this much variance between translations. In this case, due to a corruption in the Hebrew text itself, the translations either do not appear to realize numbers are missing (NKJV), try to determine what is missing (NASB, NASBU, NIV), or make a notation to reflect the missing numbers (RSV, ESV).

2. A Hebrew Bible

Most scholars agree that *Biblia Hebraica Stuttgartensia*, for size and cost, is the most useful modern Hebrew Bible.

> ☆ Elliger, K., and W. Rudolph, eds. *Biblia Hebraica Stuttgartensia.* 4th ed. Stuttgart: Deutsche Bibelgesellschaft, 1983. About $70 new, $50 used.

This is the most up-to-date Hebrew Bible that faithfully reflects the Masoretic tradition found in Codex Leningradensis (B19ᴬ), even in places where this text is known to be wrong (e.g., Gen. 4:18; Isa. 2:15; Jonah 3:6). It includes a revision of the masoretic notations along the side of the page and at the bottom (called the *Masorah parva* and the *Masorah magna* respectively; certain entries still need to be corrected). The Codex Leningradensis is the earliest complete manuscript from the Ben Asher tradition, dated to A.D. 1008 or 1009. The editors of *BHS* have compiled a textual apparatus at the bottom of the page which includes some variant readings and their evaluations. The study of Old Testament textual criticism is fascinating, and the textual apparatus at the bottom of the pages of *BHS* provides enough information to give the reader some idea about various readings in other sources. The textual apparatus in this edition is superior to the earlier one,[8] primarily because it represents far fewer textual emendations (i.e., changes in the Hebrew text without support from other sources). A fifth edition of *BHS* is in process, called *Biblia Hebraica Quinta* (*BHQ*), with completely reworked Masorah and textual notes.

3. Guides to BHS

Because much of the massive material in *BHS* is condensed and abbreviated in other languages, other books are available to assist in using it:

☆ Kelley, Page H., Daniel S. Mynatt, and Timothy G. Crawford. *The Masorah of Biblia Hebraica Stuttgartensia: Introduction and Annotated Glossary.* Grand Rapids: Eerdmans, 1998. About $26 new, $19 used.

The Kelley, Mynatt, and Crawford guide to *BHS* is very thorough and easy to use.

• Scott, William R. *A Simplified Guide to "BHS": Critical Apparatus, Masora, Accents, Unusual Letters and Other Markings.* 3rd ed. Berkeley: BIBAL, 1995. About $8 new, $6 used.

Scott's guide to *BHS* also contains much useful information and is more modestly priced.

---

8. R. Kittel, *Biblia Hebraica*, 3rd ed. (Stuttgart: Württembergische Bibelanstalt, 1937).

- Wonneberger, Reinhard. *Understanding "BHS": A Manual for the Users of Biblia Hebraica Stuttgartensia.* Translated by Dwight R. Daniels. 3rd ed. Stuttgartensia: Jesuit Consortium, 2001. About $65 new, $35 used.

The Wonneberger guide is a classic guide that summarizes the material well and is very thorough, but is difficult to find things in.

4. A Parsing Guide
There are several good options for parsing guides, but the most modern and easy-to-use is the *Old Testament Parsing Guide*:

☆ Beall, Todd S., William A. Banks, and Colin Smith. *Old Testament Parsing Guide.* Revised and updated edition. Nashville: Broadman & Holman, 2000. About $26 new, $22 used.

This guide is arranged verse-by-verse with a complete parsing of every verb. It provides brief word definitions, as well as relevant page numbers in two biblical Hebrew lexicons (i.e., BDB and *HALOT*). This allows the translator to move fairly quickly through a passage and ascertain the correct parsing for each verb—a tremendous benefit.

5. A Reading Guide
A reading guide is a quick way to access vocabulary so that a busy pastor or beginning scholar can translate fairly easily without having to look up every word in a lexicon. One such reading guide is:

☆ Brown, A. Philip and Bryan W. Smith. *A Reader's Hebrew Bible.* Grand Rapids: Zondervan, 2008. About $50 new, $25 used.

This work will save time and effort for those reading the Hebrew Bible by providing the definitions of the Hebrew and Aramaic words in footnotes at the bottom of the page. These footnotes contain context-specific meanings for each Hebrew word used less than one hundred times and each Aramaic word used less than twenty-five times.

• Armstrong, T. A., D. L. Busby, and C. F. Carr. *A Reader's Hebrew-English Lexicon of the Old Testament*. 4 Vols. Grand Rapids: Zondervan, 1989. About $50 used.

This guide is a bit more specific than the previous work by providing vocabulary and indicating how often a word is used in a particular book and in the whole Old Testament. Hebrew words occurring fifty times or fewer and Aramaic words occurring ten times or fewer are listed in sequence by chapter and verse. This guide also provides the page number of the word in BDB.

6. A Hebrew-English Lexicon

The most recent, up-to-date Hebrew lexicon for the Old Testament and related literature is based on the third edition of Koehler and Baumgartner's Hebrew lexicon in German:

☆ Koehler, L., W. Baumgartner, and J. J. Stamm. *The Hebrew and Aramaic Lexicon of the Old Testament* [*HALOT*]. Translated and edited under the supervision of M. E. J. Richardson. 5 vols. Leiden: Brill, 1994–2000. About $400 to $500 new for all five volumes; about $190 new for a two-volume study edition, about $150 used.

HALOT has been translated from the German and edited under the supervision of M. E. J. Richardson from the University of Manchester. Prepared by an international team of Hebrew and Old Testament scholars, *HALOT* takes advantage of the great strides made in the last hundred years in the field of Semitic linguistics. Words are arranged in alphabetical order, solving one of the major problems with BDB. The first four volumes cover Hebrew vocabulary and the fifth covers Aramaic. This work consults Hebrew texts from the Dead Sea area, as well as other cognate Semitic languages to try to determine possible meanings of rare Hebrew words. The process of seeking meanings of Old Testament Hebrew words from other Semitic languages is fraught with difficulties, but occasionally there is no other option.

This extensive work has two drawbacks: it is quite costly and it is cumbersome to use since the reader constantly needs to switch between volumes. The unabridged two-volume study edition (2001; about $190) and the CD ROM editions (Logos Bible Software and BibleWorks, about $160) partly address both problems. Further, the two-volume study edition matches the page numbers of the five-volume set, so there is no confusion when other materials cite *HALOT*. A final lexical tool is a condensed version of the earlier form of *HALOT*:

* Holladay, William L. *A Concise Hebrew-Aramaic Lexicon of the Old Testament.* Leiden: Brill, 1988. About $35 new, $25 used.

Holladay's condensed resource gives the various meanings of Hebrew words but does not always provide sufficient information for in-depth study.

For those who can not afford *HALOT*, an older lexicon is BDB, but it will have to be used with caution:

* Brown, Francis, S. R. Driver, and C. A. Briggs. *Hebrew and English Lexicon of the Old Testament.* Oxford: Clarendon, 1906. Corrected by G. R. Driver, Oxford: Clarendon, 1951 (about $70). Reprint, Peabody, MA: Hendrickson, 1998 (about $35 new, $16 used).

This lexicon took about twenty-three years to compile and was completed in 1907. G. R. Driver made small corrections in 1951, but its linguistic material is seriously outdated and much of the evidence from the Dead Sea Scrolls and Ugarit is not incorporated. Thus it will need to be compared to more modern resources. Much of the evidence cited from Arabic or South Arabic is dubious, since it is now commonly recognized that Arabic is a Southwest Semitic language and that Hebrew and Aramaic are Northwest Semitic languages. Thus similar words found in Arabic may not really correspond to Hebrew and Aramaic words that may look like cognates. BDB should not be used to determine a word's etymology; in fact, serious errors have occurred by those unaware of this problem.

BDB is a very thorough work with many biblical passages listed to provide the range of meanings for the various Hebrew words, and the dagger (†) at the beginning of selected articles signifies that every occurrence of the word in the Hebrew Old Testament is recorded in the article. Each entry in BDB includes the Hebrew word, its part of speech (e.g., verb, noun), gender (if applicable), various forms, and glosses, with multiple examples. Another significant problem with this lexicon is that its authors assumed nouns came from verbs. As a result, the editors placed nouns under the verbs they believed them to be related to, making it difficult to locate certain nouns. The following additional index helps to save time locating nouns in BDB:

- Einspahr, Bruce. *Index to Brown-Driver-Briggs Hebrew and English Lexicon.* Chicago: Moody, 1977. About $30 new, $15 used.

Since BDB has significant weaknesses, this next work is in the process of updating the material.

- Clines, D. J. A., ed. *The Dictionary of Classical Hebrew.* Sheffield: Sheffield Academic Press, 1988–. About $130 to $200 per volume new, difficult to find used.

The Dictionary of Classical Hebrew will include all ancient Hebrew literature, not just the Old Testament; however, it will not include any Semitic cognates. This set is beyond the budget of most pastors and students, costing about $130 to $200 per volume (eight are anticipated).

7. A Hebrew-English Concordance
This advanced Hebrew concordance by Even-Shoshan is slightly more difficult to use than the following one by Wigram, but it is well worth its price:

- ☆ Even-Shoshan, Abraham. *A New Concordance of the Bible.* 2nd ed. Grand Rapids: Baker, 1989. About $125 new, $45 used.

This resource contains information that is not available in other Hebrew concordances. In addition to listing every Hebrew and Aramaic word, including proper nouns and pronouns, in alphabetical order (שׂ ["*śîn*"] and שׁ ["*šîn*"] are listed together), it also numbers references so that it is simple to determine how often a word is used. Synonyms and collocations (i.e., words that are commonly used together) are listed for each word, with the reference numbers so they can be easily checked. John H. Sailhamer has written an extremely helpful introduction to Even-Shoshan's concordance:

- Sailhamer, John H. *Introduction to A New Concordance of the Old Testament.* Grand Rapids: Baker, 1984. About $8 new.

- *Wigram, George V. The Englishman's Hebrew Concordance of the Old Testament. Peabody, MA: Hendrickson, 1997. About $30 new, $21 used.*

I also recommend this user-friendly concordance for most pastors and Hebrew students. This standard reference work was first published in 1843. It contains every Hebrew and Aramaic word in the Old Testament in alphabetical order with an English translation of the phrase where the word occurs. The most recent edition is coded with Strong's numbering system for each word, so even those who do not know Hebrew can use it. Hebrew and English indexes also appear at the back of the book. Hebrew word studies can be done very quickly with this resource.

8. A Beginning Hebrew Grammar
In the last few years a plethora of beginning Hebrew grammars has appeared. Most likely, your Hebrew instructor chose a Hebrew grammar for you based on his or her preferences. It is generally best to continue on with the grammar that you learned Hebrew with. However, it can be helpful to get another perspective—another Hebrew grammar may explain some things more clearly or offer better and/or different examples. I will rate them here in the order of what I consider to be the easiest grammars for learning Hebrew, but all of them are useful grammars:

☆ Fuller, Russell T., and Kyoungwon Choi. *Invitation to Biblical Hebrew: A Beginning Grammar.* Grand Rapids: Kregel. 2006. About $50.

Fuller and Choi divide their book into manageable

learning sections, presenting the strong verbs first and then the weak verbs. It is particularly good at giving the keys for learning each verb form and providing exercises to learn the various principles in each chapter.

- Pratico, Gary D., and Miles V. Van Pelt. *Basics of Biblical Hebrew Grammar.* 2nd ed. Grand Rapids: Zondervan, 2007. About $45 new, $25 used.

Although the strong and weak verbs are mixed together in the lessons, Pratico and Van Pelt's grammar still contains a good explanation of the essentials of Biblical Hebrew. The included CD-ROM contains useful verb charts, overheads, answer keys to the exercises, and vocabulary helps.

- Kelley, Page H. *Biblical Hebrew: An Introductory Grammar.* Grand Rapids: Eerdmans, 1992. About $35 new, $10 used.

Kelley separates strong and weak verb forms, and the exercises in the book are excellent.[9]

I have listed some other grammars below in alphabetical order:

Blau, Joshua. *A Grammar of Biblical Hebrew.* Porta linguarum Orientalium; Neue Serie. 2nd ed. Wiesbaden: Otto Harrassowitz, 1993. About $170.

Davidson, Andrew B. *Introductory Hebrew Grammar.* Edited by James D. Martin. 27th ed. Edinburgh: T & T Clark, 1954. About $20.

Garrett, Duane A. *A Modern Grammar for Classical Hebrew.* Nashville: Broadman & Holman, 2002. About $35.

Gibson, John C. *Davidson's Introductory Hebrew Grammar-Syntax.* 4th ed. Edinburgh: T & T Clark, 1994. About $40.

---

9. See also Page H. Kelley, Terry L. Burden, and Timothy G. Crawford. *A Handbook to Biblical Hebrew: An Introductory Grammar* (Grand Rapids: Eerdmans, 1994).

Greenberg, Moshe. *Introduction to Hebrew.* Englewood, NJ: Prentice-Hall, 1965. About $50.

Hamilton, Jeffries M., Jeffrey S. Rodgers, and C. L. Seow. *A Grammar for Biblical Hebrew Handbook.* Revised edition. Nashville: Abingdon, 2002. About $42.

Harris, R. Laird. *Introductory Hebrew Grammar.* Grand Rapids: Eerdmans, 1950. About $20.

Harrison, Roland K. *Teach Yourself Biblical Hebrew.* New York: McGraw-Hill, 1991. About $50.

Hunter, A. Vanlier. *Biblical Hebrew Workbook: An Inductive Study for Beginners.* Lanham, MD: University Press of America, 1988. About $44.

Kittel, Bonnie P., et al. *Biblical Hebrew: A Text and Workbook.* Yale Language Series. New Haven: Yale University Press, 1989. About $58.

Lambdin, Thomas O. *Introduction to Biblical Hebrew.* Upper Saddle River, NJ: Prentice Hall, 1971. About $95.

Mansoor, Menahem. *Biblical Hebrew Step-by-Step.* 3rd ed. 2 volumes. Grand Rapids: Baker, 1984. About $50.

Marks, John H., and Virgil M. Rogers. *A Beginner's Handbook to Biblical Hebrew.* Nashville: Abingdon, 1958. Used about $10.

Merwe, C. H. J. van der, J. A. Naude, and J. H. Kroeze. *A Biblical Reference Grammar.* Sheffield: Sheffield Academic Press, 1999. About $30.

Rodgers, Jeffery S. *A Grammar for Biblical Hebrew Handbook.* Nashville: Abingdon, 2002. About $42.

Ross, Allen P. *Introducing Biblical Hebrew.* Grand Rapids: Baker, 2001. About $40.

Seow, Choon L. *A Grammar for Biblical Hebrew.* 2nd edition. Nashville: Abingdon, 1995. About $36.

Weingreen, J. *A Practical Grammar for Classical Hebrew.* 2nd ed. Oxford: Clarendon, 1959. About $50 new, $35 used.

9. A Vocabulary List

Another helpful tool for learning biblical Hebrew vocabulary is a list of Hebrew and Aramaic words:

☆ Van Pelt, Miles V. and Gary D. Pratico. *The Vocabulary Guide to Biblical Hebrew.* Grand Rapids: Zondervan, 2003. New about $17, used $10.

This book contains all the Old Testament Hebrew vocabulary occurring ten times or more in descending order of frequency. It helps save time by allowing the reader to learn the words that occur most frequently in the Hebrew Bible. Also along with the primary word, it will often include some Hebrew words that are related. All words are arranged according to the primary three root radicals and there is also a list of unusual and difficult words (including proper nouns, adjectives, prepositions, pronouns, particles, and verbs).

10. A Reference Hebrew Grammar
A reference Hebrew grammar is helpful for studying the more complicated Hebrew grammatical structures.

☆ Kautzsch, E. *Gesenius' Hebrew Grammar.* Translated by A. E. Cowley. 2nd ed. Oxford: Oxford University Press, 1910. About $60 new, $40 used.

Wilhelm Gesenius (1786–1842) was a pioneer in the study of Hebrew grammar and BDB (1906) is based upon his *Thesaurus* (i.e., his examination of each Hebrew word). His Hebrew grammar (*Hebräische Grammatik*) went through thirteen editions, and even after his death his work was carried on. E. Rödiger published the 14th to 21st editions, and Emil Kautzsch published the next seven editions. Kautzsch revised and enlarged the last of these seven editions to create the 28th edition, and Arthur E. Cowley published this second English edition in 1910. The grammar also contains a facsimile copy of the Siloam inscription with a translation. It has become one of the standard Hebrew reference grammars even though it is sadly dated, being almost a century old.

GKC has a wealth of information, and is one of the most comprehensive works on the Hebrew language. It contains discussions concerning Hebrew roots, derivatives, prefixes and suffixes, syntax, and pronunciation, as well as in-depth discussions of the history of the language and its syntax. One of the major drawbacks of this volume is that one may need to use linguistic dictionaries or more basic grammars to understand some of the technical discussions. The book is divided into three parts: phonology (i.e., history and theory of sound changes in a language), morphology (i.e., word formations), and syntax (i.e., the way words are combined to form clauses and sentences). The indexes in the back of the book are extremely thorough. For example, by consulting the index of passages, you can determine if there are any discussions on Genesis 3:15. (Note: the indexes use paragraph numbers and letters instead of page numbers.) James Barr comments, "This is the standard reference grammar for most serious students of Hebrew in the English-speaking world; it has been so for eighty years and looks like continuing for many more."[10]

11. A Hebrew Syntax Book

A book on Hebrew syntax provides the pastor or Hebrew student with a basic understanding of the structure of Hebrew sentences.

☆ Williams, Ronald J. *Williams' Hebrew Syntax.* Revised and expanded by John C. Beckman. 3rd ed. Toronto: University of Toronto Press, 2007. About $25 new, $17 used.

This short paperback outlines Hebrew syntax, describing the basic syntactical functions of nouns, verbs, particles, and clauses. The biblical examples provided, though sometimes unclear, are generally sufficient to explain the concept under consideration. This book is excellent for understanding how prepositions and particles can be used in Hebrew, and the index on the final pages make finding this information quite simple.

• Arnold, Bill T., and John H. Choi. *A Guide to Biblical Hebrew Syntax.* Cambridge: Cambridge University Press, 2003. About $18 new, $16 used.

Arnold and Choi's *Guide* is another very helpful Hebrew syntax book that summarizes the various aspects of Hebrew syntax with plenty of examples from the Hebrew text. It also has a very useful glossary.

---

10. James Barr, "Book Reviews: Gesenius' Hebrew Grammar," *JBL* 101 (March 1982): 138.

• Waltke, Bruce K., and M. O'Connor. *An Introduction to Biblical Hebrew Syntax.* Winona Lake, IN: Eisenbrauns, 1990. About $60 new, $55 used.

For those who want a more in-depth discussion of Hebrew syntax, Waltke and O'Connor provide it. They describe their book as an intermediate grammar to be used between basic grammatical studies and more advanced research literature. This research work provides the most up-to-date, scholarly discussion of Hebrew grammar in the English language. It is arranged by topics, including the history of the Hebrew language and the Hebrew text; the study of Hebrew grammar, linguistics, and grammatical units; nouns, adjectives, numerals, and pronouns; Classical Hebrew verbal stems; and the usage of verbal conjugations and clauses. While it does not replace a reference grammar, which treats exceptions and all aspects of grammar and syntax, its discussions are well written and thorough with more than thirty-five hundred biblical Hebrew examples and discussions of other cognate Semitic languages. Linguistic vocabulary is well explained and a helpful glossary (pp. 689–94) defines the more technical terms. Four indexes (i.e., Scripture, authorities cited, Hebrew words, and topics) make the forty chapters and almost seven hundred pages of information readily accessible. The footnotes provide good bibliographical information so you can delve more deeply into specific features of Hebrew grammar.

12. A Hebrew Word Study Dictionary
A word study dictionary provides the busy pastor or student with basic, and, in some cases, fairly advanced word studies on biblical Hebrew words. Word study dictionaries save time by providing the Semitic background of each word, specific meanings, and related Hebrew words. For most pastors and students, the best word study dictionary is VanGemeren's:

☆ VanGemeren, Willem A., ed. *New International Dictionary of Old Testament Theology and Exegesis* [*NIDOTTE*]. 5 vols. Grand Rapids: Zondervan, 1997. About $200 new, $120 used (CD-ROM version, $91).

VanGemeren's five-volume work took eight years to produce and not only includes an analysis of individual Hebrew words, but also ten detailed articles on hermeneutics and interpretation topics. It is the counterpart to Colin Brown's *New International Dictionary of New Testament Theology* (4 volumes). The first four volumes of the *NIDOTTE* include all the Hebrew words contained in the Old Testament in Hebrew alphabetical order for easy reference. Each article discusses the word's semantic cognates, similar words, meaning(s) in its Old Testament contexts, and information on post-biblical developments in the understanding of the word. An index cross-references the article numbers in *NIDOTTE* with numbers used by Strong's and Goodrick/Kohlenberger's concordances (*The Strongest NIV Exhaustive Concordance*) so that those who do not know Hebrew can even use *NIDOTTE*. At the end of volume 4, there is a topical dictionary with articles on the theology of each individual Old Testament book, as well as people, places, events, and literary topics. The last volume contains various indexes (i.e., Hebrew index, Scripture index, subject index, and an index of semantic fields) for ease of reference.

A more condensed word study dictionary is that of Harris, Archer, and Waltke:

• Harris, R. Laird, Gleason L. Archer Jr., and Bruce K. Waltke. *Theological Wordbook of the Old Testament* [*TWOT*]. Chicago: Moody, 2003. About $75 new, $40 used.

TWOT is a helpful tool to provide the meanings for Hebrew words (except names) in the Old Testament. The words are easy to find—an index in the back of volume two keys the words to Strong's concordance. Its briefer articles provide the basic meanings and uses of each Hebrew word, but brevity can be a drawback when looking for detailed information about an Old Testament word.

13. A Book on Old Testament Textual Criticism
Sometimes differences between English Bibles can cause misunderstandings and uncertainty concerning the biblical text among people in a congregation, and thus it can be helpful to have a book on textual criticism.

☆ Wegner, Paul D. *A Student's Guide to Textual Criticism of the Bible: Its History, Methods and Results.* Downers Grove, IL: InterVarsity Press, 2006. About $12 new, $10 used.

This is a practical, step-by-step guide on how to do textual criticism in both the Old and New Testaments. It explains the basic principles of textual criticism, and provides footnotes and bibliographies for further study.

• Tov, Emanuel. *Textual Criticism of the Hebrew Bible.* 2nd ed. Minneapolis: Fortress; Assen: Van Gorcum, 2001. About $54 new, $30 used.

The next level of sophistication is clearly Emanuel Tov's book on textual criticism of the Old Testament. For in-depth textual criticism of the Old Testament, Emanuel Tov is eminently qualified as an author; he is the editor-in-chief of the Dead Sea Scrolls publication project, and his specialized knowledge in the Dead Sea Scrolls and the Septuagint adds a unique depth of scholarship to this work. This is a reference work that thoroughly describes the history of the Old Testament text, its copying and transmission, as well as many of its textual problems. Although lacking a glossary of terms, the illustrative plates help the reader better grasp the complexities of this area of study.

14. A Septuagint

☆ Brenton, Lancelot C. L. *The Septuagint Version of the Old Testament and Apocrypha with an English Translation.* 1851. Reprint, Peabody, MA: Hendrickson, 1986. About $45 new, $27 used.

The Brenton edition of the Septuagint has one of the most helpful formats for pastors and students who wish to keep up their Greek. It contains the Greek text with a parallel (not interlinear) English translation by Brenton. One of its major drawbacks is that it was originally published in 1851. Since then, new and better Greek manuscripts have been discovered and our knowledge of certain Greek words has improved. Still, with Brenton's helpful textual and translational footnotes, this is a great resource for scholars and laypeople alike.

- Rahlfs, Alfred, ed. *Septuaginta, id est Vetus Testamentum graece iuxta LXX Interpretes.* 2 vols. Stuttgart: Württembergische Bibelanstalt, 1935. Reprint, New York: American Bible Society, 1979. About $50 new, $40 used.

To move to the next level of study, a more up-to-date copy of the Septuagint is the popular edition by Alfred Rahlfs (1865–1935). His personal goal was to reconstruct the original wording of the Septuagint. By the time of his death only one critical volume (*Psalmi cum Odis*) and two slim volumes on the books of Ruth and Genesis were completed; however, others carried on his work. This is an abridged critical edition of the Septuagint using primarily three manuscripts: Codex Vaticanus (B, 4th century A.D.); Codex Sinaiticus (א, 4th century A.D.); and Codex Alexandrinus (A, 5th century A.D.). A brief textual apparatus appears at the bottom of each page.

PART II: ADDING TO YOUR LIBRARY

In addition to language tools, a pastor needs to have resources that provide Old Testament background. These tools can also help you determine the meaning of specific passages or identify concepts in the Old Testament, and they can be added to your library more slowly. These works are extremely useful and offer good value for your money.

1. A Bible Encyclopedia

Bible encyclopedias provide good summary articles or overviews of specific topics.

☆ Freedman, David N., ed. *Anchor Bible Dictionary.* 6 vols. New York: Doubleday, 1992. About $250 new, $230 used.

The *ABD* set is one of the most recent and thorough Bible encyclopedias. Its authors were chosen as specialists in their various fields, whether evangelical or not, and thus readers will find a wide range of scholarly views. *ABD*'s bibliographies guide readers who wish to do further research on a topic.

2. A Bible Atlas
   Sometimes knowing the geography of the biblical lands or the location of a particular city can help provide insight into a passage. This type of information can be found in a good Bible atlas.

> ☆ Aharoni, Yohanan, Michael Avi-Yonah, Anson F. Rainey, and Ze'ev Safrai. *The Macmillan Bible Atlas.* 3rd ed. New York: Macmillan, 1993. This work is now called *The Carta Bible Atlas.* 4th edition. Jerusalem: Carta, 2002. About $40 new, $30 used.

The discussions and detailed maps of this atlas are excellent. It also provides detailed notes on the geographical locations, military campaigns, major trade routes, and archaeological sites, as well as a place index and a new name index. One drawback is that the illustrations are two-color maps or black-and-white line drawings instead of satellite pictures like those in the NET Bible (www.bible.org).

3. An Old Testament Introduction

> ☆ Harrison, Roland K. *Introduction to the Old Testament.* Grand Rapids: Eerdmans, 1969. About $20 new or used.

Harrison's one-volume introduction is probably one of the most thorough and complete available. It provides extensive background material for each biblical book and highlights special problems for each. It begins with a discussion of the JEDP theory and Harrison's arguments against it. Other areas discussed include archaeology, chronology, the Old Testament canon, and Old Testament history and religion. This work is an amazing compendium for serious study of the Hebrew Bible.

4. An Old Testament Survey
   There are many good Old Testament survey books for students of varying levels of expertise. Although I recommend

two here, be aware that there are a number of other quality options. The two listed here provide excellent overviews of the Old Testament books, highlighting important issues within each and providing questions for further study.

College Level

> ☆ Arnold, Bill T., and Bryan E. Beyer. *Encountering the Old Testament: A Christian Survey.* 2nd ed. Grand Rapids: Baker, 2008. About $50 new, $22 used.

Seminary Level

> ☆ Hill, Andrew E., and John H. Walton. *A Survey of the Old Testament.* 2nd ed. Grand Rapids: Zondervan, 2000. About $35 new, $20 used.

5. *An Old Testament History*
   Here again there are several good histories of the Old Testament.

> ☆ Merrill, Eugene H. *A Kingdom of Priests: A History of Old Testament Israel.* 2nd ed. Grand Rapids: Baker, 2008. About $24 new.

Merrill's book provides a thorough and lucid history of Israel from a conservative viewpoint.

> • Miller, J. Maxwell, and John H. Hayes. *A History of Ancient Israel and Judah.* 2nd ed. Louisville: Westminster John Knox, 2006. About $27 new, $14 used.

Although certain views in Miller and Hayes's book run counter to a conservative, evangelical perspective, this book is useful from the standpoint that it skillfully integrates ancient Near Eastern material with biblical material.

6. *A Chart Book*

> ☆ Walton, John H. *Chronological and Background*

Charts of the Old Testament. 2nd ed. Grand Rapids: Zondervan, 1994. About $14 new, $8 used.

Walton's chart book contains about one hundred charts that compile a wide array of information in a brief, easy-to-access format. In the second edition, Walton added forty-two new charts and revised eighteen others. These charts cover specific historical, literary, archaeological, and theological issues of the Old Testament.

7. Old Testament Commentaries
It is crucial to have a good collection of commentaries for Old Testament study and exposition. Not only are most pastors and students less familiar with the Old Testament, but experts are needed to unravel some of the difficulties found there. Frederick W. Danker observes:

> Expositors who think they can work independently of commentators display not only consummate arrogance but also ignorance of the conditions that obtain in biblical studies. The many areas of specialty require great leisure for properly assessing and evaluating the many discoveries, investigations, and modes of inquiry that may lead to light on a dark portion of the Bible. Such leisure few can lavish. Moreover, Scripture does not always reveal its secrets in the same measure to each generation, much less to every expositor. Interpretive sensitivity is required; people like Chrysostom, Luther, Calvin, Bengel, Westcott, Lightfoot, and others had it. To deprive oneself of an encounter with such princely blood is to impoverish oneself.[11]

Commentaries are expensive and numerous. The following guidelines should help you choose where to invest your money:

A. I recommend exegetical commentaries (i.e., those that explain passages verse-by-verse or by groups of

---

11. Frederick W. Danker, *Multipurpose Tools for Bible Study*, 2nd ed. (Minneapolis: Augsburg Fortress, 2003), 305–6.

verses) over homiletical commentaries (i.e., those that offer suggestions for preaching the passage). The latter type often lack sufficient insight into biblical passages. I have found that if you have a good understanding of the history, background, and meaning of the passage, it is fairly easy to preach it. For a good article that provides an excellent overview of the various approaches found in commentaries, see William B. Badke, "Varieties of the Biblical Commentary: A Guide to Form and Function" (this article does not list many commentaries by name).[12]

B. It is generally not the best use of your money to buy complete series of commentaries, since individual commentaries in every series vary in quality. However, should you choose a single series, I recommend the Tyndale Old Testament Commentary Series. Published in paperback, it is reasonably priced and provides a good general overview in a verse-by-verse format. One volume in the series is:

• Harrison, Roland K. *Jeremiah and Lamentations*. Tyndale Old Testament Commentaries. Downers Grove, IL: InterVarsity Press, 1981. About $12 new, $5 used. The Tyndale Old Testament Commentary Series is finally complete and costs about $340 new; the New Testament series runs about $230.

C. It is better to buy the best commentaries on specific books and then grow into them. These should be research quality, written by someone who is an expert on that specific book.

D. Buy commentaries when you need them and when you are ready to use them. When you are doing a study on the Psalms, that is a good time to go to a library where you can look through various commentaries on the Psalms and see which best fits your

---

12. William B. Badke, "Varieties of the Biblical Commentary: A Guide to Form and Function," *The Christian Librarian* 30 (February 1987): 31–35.

purposes. In addition to the chart of recommended commentaries in appendix A, the following books can also help you determine which commentaries are best:

• Glynn, John. *Commentary and Reference Survey: A Comprehensive Guide to Biblical and Theological Resources.* 10th ed. Grand Rapids: Kregel, 2007.

• Longman, Tremper, III. *Old Testament Commentary Survey.* 4th ed. Grand Rapids: Baker, 2007.

While commentaries will be your most expensive investment, they are almost certainly the best investment. Gleaning information from them will improve your sermons, and they will help you stay current on important issues in Old Testament scholarship.

PART III: COMPUTER SOFTWARE

There are a number of good tools available as software. Missionaries and others who may move frequently will benefit from computerized tools. Before investing in software, however, you need to assess how comfortable you are with computers and whether your computer system can support it. Some biblical tools that are free on the Internet can provide good search capabilities. Other software tools can be quite expensive and require significant training in order to use them effectively. With this in mind, choose software carefully, and before you make a purchase, be sure you know someone who can help answer questions that may arise.

1. Free Bible Software and Web-based Tools

There are many free programs that do biblical searches and that contain several Bible translations. These programs generally use older lexicons and tools, and therefore their information is in the public domain. I mention here some popular free tools that are valuable for quick biblical searches.

• *Blue Letter Bible* (http://blueletterbible.org)

Blue Letter Bible can search several translations using words, phrases, and Strong's numbers. It has six Bible encyclopedias and dictionaries that are fully searchable, as well as maps and images. Its developers have added an institute featuring several pastors (e.g., Ray Stedman) who teach courses available in MP3 format. The Web site has some nice maps and images. While this is a good free tool, it has limited value for pastors and students who know Hebrew.

- *Crosswalk.com* (http://www.crosswalk.com)
This freeware includes a parallel Bible format and an interlinear. It contains about twenty-seven different Bible translations and has significant search capabilities. Once again, most of Crosswalk's resources are older and thus in public domain. For the Old Testament, it includes BDB and is keyed to *TWOT*. Additionally, it has a section with illustrations that may be helpful for sermon preparation (you can e-mail up to seven illustrations to yourself per week for free, then more illustrations for a nominal charge).

- *Crosswire* (http://www.crosswire.org)
The SWORD Project is Crosswire Bible Society's free Bible software project. This Web site is for Christian computer programmers who want to help create new Bible tools. Their purpose is "to create cross-platform open-source tools, covered by the GNU General Public License, that allow programmers and Bible societies to write new Bible software more quickly and easily. Its secondary purpose is to amass a library of Bibles and other Scripture-related texts that can be used by all SWORD Project-based software."[13] Crosswire includes more than two dozen English Bible translations, a number of foreign language Bibles, several Greek and Hebrew texts, and the Septuagint text. The site does not include many lexicons, commentaries, or tools, but has powerful search capabilities.

- *E-sword* (http://www.e-sword.net)
This free software has approximately nine Bible translations and seven older research works. It is easy to use

---

13. Crosswire, http://www. crosswire.org/index.jsp (accessed March 25, 2006).

and performs simple word searches. Hebrew and Greek capabilities are limited, but you can search words using Strong's numbering system. E-sword has several Greek New Testament texts and an unpointed Hebrew Old Testament (containing Strong's numbers). Its strongest features are a parallel Bible format, the ability for the reader to add their own notes to the text, and charts and maps.

2. Purchased Bible Software

While free Bible software can help you a great deal, some capabilities you will find only in purchased software. Generally these software bundles contain several modern resources that enhance the software's usefulness.

• *QuickVerse* ($60 to $800)

QuickVerse is a very popular Bible study program and can search biblical texts and tools fairly quickly. The data in the chart are based on QuickVerse 2008 for Windows, but there is also (more limited) software for Mac, palms, and pocket PCs.

QUICKVERSE		
EDITION	COST	FEATURES
Essentials	$60	10 Bible translations and 65 reference tools
Standard	$130	14 Bible translations and 94 reference tools
Expanded	$250	16 Bible translations and 126 reference tools
Deluxe	$350	21 Bible translations and 181 reference tools
Platinum	$800	25 Bible translations and 275 reference tools

QuickVerse will facilitate basic word searches; however, its reference works are of limited value for study purposes, primarily because they are older. QuickVerse allows you to create your own "books" that can be synchronized by biblical book, chapter, and verse—a potentially useful tool for creating notes and sermons. There are no Hebrew capabilities in the program, and the tools for research are meager.

- *eBible* ($50 to $400)
  Nelson Electronic Publishing has produced an easy-to-use Bible software which imitates how programs work on the Internet. Its one-click technology can create word studies, reports, lists, and much more. By using Libronix software, it is compatible with many of the major modern resource tools.

EBIBLE		
EDITION	COST	FEATURES
Discover	$50	5 Bible translations and 18 reference tools (e.g., Matthew Henry's Commentary, New Nave's Topical Bible, Nelson's New Illustrated Bible Dictionary)
Standard	$100	7 Bible translations and 32 reference tools
Deluxe	$180	7 Bible translations and 90 reference tools
Platinum	$400	10 Bible translations and more than 150 reference tools

The Platinum Edition includes the Greek and Hebrew texts, dictionaries, and semantic domain materials. Although *eBible* uses Strong's Greek and Hebrew numbers to search through the biblical texts and other sources, it can still provide quick basic searches. Access to Louw-Nida's *Dictionary of Biblical Languages with Semantic Domains* is a great benefit of this software (only in the Platinum Edition).

- *PC Study Bible* ($50 to $900)
  This software has similar capabilities to the *eBible* software above, with the same limitations in using Strong's numbers for searches, except *PC Study Bible* is somewhat

better than *eBible* for Old Testament studies (e.g., includes a Hebrew Bible and some Hebrew resource tools). *PC Study Bible* contains some helpful works, but most are of limited value for working in Hebrew. The data in the chart below are based on PC Study Bible Version 5.

PC STUDY BIBLE		
EDITION	COST	FEATURES
Discovery	$50	13 Bible translations and 51 reference tools
New	$125	15 Bible translations and 63 reference tools
Plus	$250	18 Bible translations and 78 reference tools
Complete	$400	23 Bible translations and 102 reference tools (including Louw-Nida), as well as Greek and Hebrew Bibles
Advanced	$600	28 Bible translations and 127 reference tools
Professional	$900	31 Bible translations and 147 reference tools

• *Accordance* ($40 to $2,500)

This is an excellent program for Macintosh computers with capabilities for highly detailed Bible searches in both Greek and Hebrew. The add-on works are seamlessly integrated into the program. Those who wish to use the program on a PC can purchase an emulator but the program will run slightly slower. The $250 Scholar's Core Bundle is a good value.

ACCORDANCE		
EDITION	COST	FEATURES
Starter Collection	$40	2 Bible translations (i.e., KJV, WEB) and 7 reference tools

ACCORDANCE (CONTINUED)		
EDITION	COST	FEATURES
Library 7: Introductory	$80	9 Bible translations and 45 reference tools
Library 7: Standard	$180	14 Bible translations and 66 reference tools
Library 7: Premier	$280	14 Bible translations and 103 reference tools
Scholar's Collection	$250	Core bundle of resources, but still need to purchase up-to-date lexicons and other helpful add-ons for additional prices (e.g., *ABD* $240; BDAG $130; *HALOT* $160; Accordance Bible Atlas $90)
Jewish Collection: Introductory	$90	Parallel viewing of Hebrew texts and translations, as well as other study tools
Jewish Collection: Advanced	$260	3 English translations of the OT, the Mishnah, Josephus, and other reference tools
Catholic Collection: Introductory	$100	Catholic Bibles, a catechism, and other study tools
Catholic Collection: Advanced	$160	Adds the Latin Vulgate, Council of Trent, and other reference tools

Users can add the newest Hebrew and Greek lexicons, Septuagint texts, and Dead Sea Scrolls to this program. The program is easy to use—passing the cursor over a word automatically brings up its lexical form, parsing information, and English definitions. It easily searches and compares Bible translations; highlights specific words or texts; and allows you to add notes, consult Greek or Hebrew lexicons, and access commentaries. There are more than two hundred Bible texts and research works; the Accordance Bible Atlas is especially good.

• *Gramcord Bible Software* ($100 to $235)
Gramcord is a powerful Bible software research program for Windows that uses the original languages to search the Hebrew and Greek texts, as well as the Septuagint and many English translations. Its search capabilities and format make arranging parallel Greek/Hebrew texts, lexicons, and dictionaries very easy. In addition, users can simply cut and paste all texts into their word processing program.

Its primary original language databases are developed and officially maintained by the three leading morphology projects: TGI (The Gramcord Institute), Westminster (Westminster Hebrew Morphology), and University of Pennsylvania/CCAT (Center for Computer Analysis of Texts). Gramcord has produced top quality tools that focus particularly on Greek and Hebrew instruction (e.g., *GreekFlash Pro* [$35], *GreekMaster* [$39], *Hammoreh Hebrew Grammar Tutorial* [$45]). Gramcord also offers an option for handheld devices.

GRAMCORD BIBLE SOFTWARE		
EDITION	COST	FEATURES
Greek NT & NAS95 Bundle	$99	3 Bible translations, the GNT, and more
Greek NT/LXX Bundle	$149	Similar to Scholar's Bundle below, but no Hebrew modules except NASB's Hebrew Dictionary
GNT/HMT/LXX Scholar's Special Bundle	$195	Adds to the $99 bundle both BHS and Gramcord's MT, LXX, lexicons, and a choice of two additional Bible translations
Ultimate Bundle	$235	10 Bible translations and 10 reference tools (including Louw-Nida)

• *BibleWorks 7* ($359 to $1500)
BibleWorks is an amazing research program for those wanting to conduct in-depth research in the original

languages. It has one hundred twelve Bible translations in thirty languages, fourteen original language texts with eighteen morphological databases, twelve Greek lexicons and dictionaries, five Hebrew lexicons and dictionaries, and thirty practical reference works. Its goal is to provide quality original language tools, and its search capabilities provide the pastor, student, or scholar all the necessary tools for serious scholarly research. While the programmers do not intend to add commentaries to the software, they continue to improve and update its original language tools.

This research tool can quickly perform everything from a simple word or phrase search to very complex morphological searches, such as finding all the occurrences of the Granville Sharp construction in the Greek texts. Users can add to the program the most up-to-date lexicons, wordbooks, and Bible encyclopedias. This program is probably best for the busy pastor who wants to keep up with current scholarship and do solid biblical research, but still has other access to a library with scholarly biblical commentaries. The information below is based on data for BibleWorks 7.

BIBLEWORKS 7		
EDITION	COST	FEATURES
Main Package	$350	
Add-ons	$135	A Greek-English Lexicon, 9th ed. (Liddell, Scott, Jones, and McKenzie)
	$43	An Introduction to Biblical Hebrew Syntax (Waltke and O'Connor)
	$15	Biblical Greek (Zerwick)
	$25	Beginning Biblical Hebrew (Futato)
	$119	Exegetical Dictionary of the New Testament (Balz and Schneider)

BIBLEWORKS 7 (CONTINUED)		
EDITION	**COST**	**FEATURES**
Add-ons (continued)	$30	Greek Grammar Beyond the Basics: An Exegetical Syntax of the New Testament (Wallace)
	$55	Greek Grammar of the New Testament and Other Early Christian Literature (Blass, Debrunner, and Funk)
	$125 $197	BDAG (if combined with *HALOT*)
	$45	New Testament Greek Manuscripts (Swanson)
	$49	Practical Grammar for Classical Hebrew, 2nd ed. (Weingreen)
	$80	Qumran Sectarian Manuscripts (Abegg)
	$159 $197	*HALOT* (if combined with BDAG)
	$30	The Text of the Earliest NT Greek Manuscripts (Comfort and Barrett)
	$59	Theological Dictionary of the New Testament, Abridged (Kittel, Friedrich, and Bromiley)
	$25	Vocabulary of the Greek New Testament (Moulton and Milligan)

- *Logos Bible Software* ($150 to $1,380)

Logos Bible Software 3 is faster and more user-friendly than previous versions, containing many research tools, commentaries, and Bible dictionaries. It can provide the most resources at your fingertips, but it can be extremely slow. However, a useful option for Logos 3 is a speed search. Another way to make this software faster is to set it up so that it will only search specific collections. The Libronix software engine allows the various collections of texts to interact seamlessly.

The instant library of Logos includes many works that have limited value and slow down the program. The Scholar's edition contains most of the resources that a pastor or student will need, but most will want to enhance it with *HALOT* and BDAG. This program will be most beneficial for missionaries and pastors without access to a good library or who move frequently. Logos's programmers continually add new commentaries and Bible resources to the collections. This program is probably best for a pastor or student who is computer savvy and would prefer using a computer over books. It integrates the resources well and users can add good commentaries easily (though not cheaply) to it. The data below are based on Logos Bible Software 3:

LOGOS BIBLE SOFTWARE 3		
EDITION	COST	FEATURES
Christian Home Library	$150	11 Bible translations and 57 reference tools
Bible Study Library	$260	18 Bible translations and 152 reference tools
Leader's Library	$309	18 Bible translations and 232 reference tools
Original Languages Library	$416	9 Bible translations and 121 reference tools
Scholar's Library	$630	19 Bible translations (same as Leader's Library, plus Wuest's Expanded NT) and 312 reference tools
Scholar's Library: Silver	$1,000	20 Bible translations and 501 reference tools
Scholar's Library: Gold	$1,308	21 Bible translations and 679 reference tools

3. Collections of Illustrations
When you have spent so much time researching and understanding a biblical text in the original languages, you want to be able to communicate it clearly and powerfully to your congregation. One tool that can help you in this area

is the use of vivid illustrations. Illustrations suitable for sermons can be accessed for free from a number of Web sites. Some sites are arranged topically and many also provide illustrations based on specific books and texts. Below I have listed what I consider to be some of the better sites:

Free Web Sites
- http://www.bible.org/illus.asp

- http://www.crosswalk.com/faith/illustration.asp (up to seven free per week)

- http://www.higherpraise.com/illustrations/a.htm

- http://elbourne.org/sermons

- http://www.sermoncentral.com (some free, some require a fee); also found at http://www.sermon illustrator.org

- http://www.sermonillustrations.com (I believe this site is the best and easiest to use.)

- http://www.sermons.org/illustrations.html

Fee-based Web Sites
- http://www.preachingtoday.com

- http://www.sermons.com

CONCLUSION

A wise old pastor friend once told me, "To be a good pastor, you need the brain of an Einstein, the skin of a rhinoceros, and the heart of a child." He's right, but since most of us are not as naturally gifted as Einstein, we can use tools to help us increase our abilities. Those who preach God's Word have a high calling to fulfill—people's lives depend upon it and we must do our job to the best of our abilities. One day we will give an account to our heavenly Father as to how we used our gifts and calling for Him. At the end of time I want to hear, "Well done, good and faithful servant, you were faithful over a few things, I will put you over many things; enter into the joy of your master" (Matt. 25:23).

THINGS TO CONSIDER

Be sure to think through the following questions about your future ministry before proceeding to the next chapter:

1. Which tools do I already have and which do I need to buy?

2. Should I invest in a computer program, and if I do, will I spend the time needed to learn how to use it?

3. How can I improve my study time?

4. Where am I losing time or using it less efficiently?

5. Can I delegate any responsibilities to others to allow more time for study?

FURTHER READING

Badke, William B. "Varieties of the Biblical Commentary: A Guide to Form and Function." *The Christian Librarian* 30 (February 1987): 31–35.

Craddock, Fred B. *Preaching.* Nashville: Abingdon, 1985. See especially pages 69–83.

Danker, Frederick W. *Multipurpose Tools for Bible Study.* 2nd ed. Minneapolis: Augsburg Fortress, 2003.

Glynn, John. *Commentary and Reference Survey: A Comprehensive Guide to Biblical and Theological Resources.* 10th ed. Grand Rapids: Kregel, 2007.

Longman, Tremper. *Old Testament Commentary Survey.* 4th ed. Grand Rapids: Baker, 2007.

Parker, Don. *Using Biblical Hebrew in Ministry: A Practical Guide for Pastors, Seminarians, and Bible Students.* Lanham, MD; New York; London: University Press of America, 1995. See especially pages 39–61.

CHAPTER
THREE

THE GOALS
OF BIBLICAL
EXEGESIS

WHAT AM I LOOKING FOR
AND HOW DO I FIND IT?

*I study my Bible like I gather apples. First, I shake
the whole tree that the ripest may fall. Then I shake
each limb, and when I have shaken each limb, I
shake each branch and every twig. Then I look
under every leaf. I search the Bible as a whole like
shaking the whole tree. Then I shake every limb—
study book after book. Then I shake every branch,
giving attention to the chapters. Then I shake every
twig, or a careful study of the paragraphs and
sentences and words and their meanings.*

—Martin Luther

Expounding God's Word is likely the most important
thing pastors do, even though many in the congregation may not realize it. Of course, it is very important

---

Epigraph. Martin Luther, http://www.sermon illustrations.com/a-z/b/
bible_study_of.htm (accessed August 22, 2006). See also *D. Martin
Luthers Werke, Kritische Gesamtausgabe*, Tischreden, 6 vols. (Weimar:
Verlag Hermann Böhlaus Nochfolger, 1912–21), 2:1877.

to visit the sick, be present when someone has lost a loved one, or visit an elderly person in your congregation, since this is how we show God's love and earn a hearing for His Word. But it is only through a constant exposure to Scripture week after week that people are changed and molded ever so gradually into more Christlike individuals. Unless people are growing spiritually, more problems are being created within the congregation than are being resolved. The Word of God acts a bit like sandpaper removing the imperfections and blemishes until we better resemble God's character. It even comes with a promise: "All Scripture is God breathed and useful for teaching, for reproof, for correction, for training in righteousness; so that the person of God may be fully equipped for every good work" (2 Tim. 3:16–17).

Increasingly, the Sunday morning worship service is becoming the primary preaching or teaching time in a church. This being the case, the Sunday morning sermon is extremely important and demands careful thought and attention. How can we best meet the needs of our congregations and provide a biblically based foundation to face life's difficult demands? What is the best way to present biblical truths in a meaningful way? I believe the answer lies in clearly formulated expository sermons in which a pastor carefully works through various books of the Bible, systematically explains (or exposits) the meaning of particular passages of Scripture, and highlights crucial elements that can be applied to the lives of his listeners. An expository sermon differs from topical preaching which concentrates on specific topics and discusses various verses relating to the topics. Topical sermons have their place, but a systematic exposition of biblical books will help the congregation understand the flow of various books and provide a more thorough biblical foundation. Walter Kaiser commonly quips that pastors may decide to preach topical sermons once in a while, but afterward let them repent and go back to preaching expository sermons.

WHAT IS EXEGESIS?

An expository sermon rises and falls on exegesis. Exegesis involves a thorough, analytical study of a biblical passage in order to develop a useful interpretation of the passage.[1] Before we can preach any passage, we need to thoroughly understand it; exegesis is the process by which we determine the meaning. Most scholars agree that this is the goal of exegesis, but few scholars agree on the best way to accomplish it. At the very least, Richard Averbeck is correct when he argues that the Old Testament text has three major dimensions: literary, historical, and theological,[2] although there is certainly overlap in these areas. A careful analysis of these elements and how they work together provides a solid foundation for understanding the Old Testament text in its original context—we call this the historical-cultural understanding of the biblical text. In sermon preparation, a pastor has to be somewhat of a generalist to assess these three dimensions. The literary dimension encompasses literary genres (e.g., prose vs. poetry), structures (e.g., chiasms, polystrophes, figures of speech), discourse analysis, and the composition of the text. The historical dimension takes note of references to people, places, events, relevant archaeological findings, ancient Near Eastern cultures and manners, the transmission of the text, the nature of historiography, and even linguistics and the meanings of words. All of this information is then brought to bear upon the theological dimension which deals with the development of presuppositions and beliefs concerning the themes of God, land, people, covenant, as well as many others, and the coherence of these ideas throughout the canon of Scripture. Each dimension deals with different issues, but each is necessary.

These three dimensions of Scripture can be examined by asking four questions. The first two deal with meaning and the last two with significance:

1. What are the broader and immediate contexts? (literary analysis)

2. What did the text mean? (historical analysis)

---

1. Douglas Stuart, *Old Testament Exegesis: A Handbook for Students and Pastors*, 3rd ed. (Louisville: Westminster John Knox, 2001), 1.
2. Richard E. Averbeck, "Factors in Reading the Patriarchal Narratives: Literary, Historical, and Theological Dimensions," in *Giving the Sense: Understanding and Using Old Testament Historical Texts*, ed. David M. Howard Jr. and Michael A. Grisanti (Grand Rapids: Kregel, 2003), 116–17.

3. How does this meaning fit into the larger picture of Scripture? (theological analysis)

4. How do we apply this text?

Exegeting a biblical passage can be compared to restoring an old car. For a complete restoration project, the car enthusiast must start with a complete dismantling of the car and an examination of each part to make sure it is working properly. The mechanic must understand each of the parts and have a good understanding of how they all fit together. This is similar to asking general questions about the text, such as, What is the larger context of this passage? This would be similar to asking, What are we working with here—a Ford or a Chevy? How does it tie into the rest of Scripture? What type of motor do we want and how will it work with the transmission? What place does it have in God's progressive revelation?

Next, the restorer starts examining in detail each part of the car. Does it have any parts that are broken, aren't working well, or just need to be cleaned and oiled? This would be like examining in more detail the near context, asking questions like: What type of literary genre is it? What is its purpose? To whom was it written and when?

After the car has been disassembled and each part checked carefully, now it is time to start putting it back together. As the car once again starts to take shape, the mechanic needs to be sure the parts fit together and that everything is working properly. Sometimes even specialists need to be called in to work on the motor or to finish the wiring. This is similar to the detailed work necessary to determine what the biblical text is saying. Examining commentaries, lexicons, or grammar books may help provide the necessary historical background or understanding of grammar that helps make sense of the passage. What does each specific Hebrew word mean? Are there any specific grammatical forms or literary arrangements that help us understand the text better? Are there any questions about the original text itself?

In the final stages of restoration the car must be painted, the interior redone, and finally reassembled. This is somewhat similar to the final stages of exegesis, where the exegete examines the theological content and determines how it applies today. What is God trying to tell us through this passage and how does it fit with the rest of Scripture?

But a car restoration project is not complete until a person gets in and starts to use it, as it should be with a biblical text. The climax of exegesis is when the meaning of the biblical passage comes across so clearly and in such specific ways that the reader or listener is motivated to modify their behavior in light of the passage.

IS ALL THIS NECESSARY?

The process of exegesis is hard work. Natural talent provides a significant advantage when you are presenting the sermon, but there is no substitute for good, hard work when preparing a sermon from the biblical text. At times the research may be tedious, but the results of this hard work can be very exciting and a powerful agent of change in people's lives.

People sometimes ask me, "Is all this necessary in order to preach God's Word?" Someone can in fact preach sermons without knowing how to do detailed exegesis. But just as there are skills and training that set apart an amateur from a competent, licensed professional, there is also training that can enable someone in ministry to handle God's Word in a skilled manner. We would never let an incompetent electrician wire our house; there is similar potential for damage should an unskilled preacher handle the Word of God.

There is also a tendency today for churches to be so seeker-sensitive that sermons can become "Bible Lite." However, these types of sermons do not meet people's needs for very long. People are longing for a real spiritual foundation and not just nice thoughts from the Bible. A recent *Time* magazine article pointed out that young people are being drawn to churches that provide solid biblical teaching and not "watered down religious content."[3]

When we stand up to teach people from God's Word, it is imperative that we be thoroughly prepared, because the spiritual lives of our people depend upon their understanding of God's Word. It is hard for a pastor to know how many corners can be cut before a good understanding of the passage is lost. In many industries, cutting corners has been

---

3. Sonja Steptoe, "In Touch with Jesus: Sugarcoated, MTV-style youth ministry is over. Bible-based worship is packing teens in pews now," *Time*, November 6, 2006, 58.

associated with reduced quality and/or safety. Cutting corners in the short-term can often end up being more costly in the long-term. So it is in quality of ministry.

If you do your work well and study the passages to the best of your ability, God will use your hard work to teach others more about Him. There are times when I've heard things in a sermon that I knew were incorrect. I wondered how the preacher got that interpretation from the passage. Times like those remind me how important the job of a pastor is. A congregation's understanding of Scripture often is only as good as their pastor's. I have never heard of a person getting in trouble for knowing God's Word too well, but the opposite is often true.

STEPS TO UNDERSTANDING SCRIPTURE

Before we can do exegesis well, we must understand the process and we must know the goals and significance of each step. In the sections below I follow the three dimensions of exegesis identified earlier: literary, historical, and theological. I then briefly describe the steps, explaining why they are important, and suggesting the types of questions to ask at each step.

Literary Analysis

The Bible is literature, and we can assume its human authors wrote with purpose; the exegete's job is to determine the purpose behind the words. Literary analysis usually begins with the larger context of a passage (i.e., the chapter and book) and then deals with the immediate context of specific paragraphs or verses.

1. Broader Context

To understand a specific text, you need to know how it fits in its larger context. Ask questions like: How does this section relate to the surrounding paragraphs, chapters, and the book as a whole? Does it provide reasons, further development, or an explanation of the previous passage(s)? Does the author use literary structures to add to the meaning? A careful literary analysis of the passage is vital for accurate exposition.[4] It can be tempting to read a single line or

---

4. A helpful resource for determining literary structures is David A. Dorsey, *The Literary Structure of the Old Testament: A Commentary on Genesis-Malachi* (Grand Rapids: Baker, 2004).

even a paragraph from the Bible and make application for today without regard to its context—something we would not typically do with any other literary work such as a play or a novel. For example, can 2 Chronicles 7:14 be directly applied to modern America when it says, "if My people who are called by My name will humble themselves and pray and seek My face and turn from their evil ways, then I myself will hear from heaven, will forgive their sin, and will heal their land"? This passage is directed specifically to the nation of Israel and thus the promise of forgiving their sins and healing their land may not directly apply to America. At the very least, 2 Chronicles 7:14 cannot be viewed as a guarantee that even if every Christian in America prayed for their country, it would be healed of its sin. However, there is certainly a general principle in Scripture that when Christians humble themselves and pray, God will hear them (e.g., Pss. 5:2; 32:6; Matt. 6:5–6; Mark 11:24; Rom. 8:26; Eph. 6:18; 1 Thess. 5:17; James 5:16), but we must leave the results up to God.

Reading verses in context is the best way to guard against "prooftexting," or forcing an incorrect meaning upon a text. Prooftexting is not only inexcusable, but it also models poor hermeneutical methods to your congregation.

Various types of criticism can help you examine the literary nature of a text in its broader and then in its more immediate contexts:

Source Criticism (sometimes called Literary Criticism): The goal of source criticism is to break a text into its original components (the pieces that the author assembled into the final work) and identify the intentions of each component. This may be somewhat similar to watching a company's PowerPoint presentation concerning its insurance benefits to its employees that is a combined effort from the insurance, human resource, and accounting departments, and then trying to determine which departments were responsible for each part of the presentation and the purpose or motivation behind each part. It has been commonly used to determine the various sources behind the Pentateuch. While modern scholars are becoming less and less certain about such endeavors, there may be more promise in other areas. For example, it appears that embedded in the Isaianic memoir of chapters 6–9 is a historical royal annal (history recorded for a king) in chapter 7. Is it possible that Isaiah had already written this annal for the king (see 2 Chron. 26:22) and decided to add it here? In general, source criticism will be used in sermon preparation only occasionally when it is useful to know how an Old Testament text was put together.

Form Criticism: Form criticism involves identifying the genre or subgenre of texts, and more specifically, examining the typical ways people would have expressed themselves for specific purposes. In contemporary terms, form criticism of a newspaper would yield such forms as classified ads, editorials, letters to the editor, human interest, news, comic strips, and satire. Each of these has a particular structure and purpose, and we read them accordingly. In Old Testament studies, forms can include such things as legends, hymns, curses, and laments. Some of the best examples of the importance of form criticism can be seen in recognizing specific types of psalms like: individual lament psalms, psalms of thanksgiving, psalms of trust, or psalms of praise. These often have a set structure that the exegete needs to recognize. For example, a psalm of praise commonly has the following structure:

1. Introductory call to praise
2. Main body (God's attributes or deeds)
3. Conclusion: Wish, prayer, blessing, praise

Psalm 8 is an interesting psalm of praise which begins with an introductory call to praise (v. 1a), followed by the main body that gives reasons why God deserves praise (vv. 1b–8), and ends with a final call to praise God (v. 9). The introductory call to praise and the conclusion are exactly the same; however in verse 1 the praises to God are anticipatory and in verse 9 they are celebratory based upon the reasons given just prior. This repetitive structure is called an inclusio and helps delimit the parameters of the psalm.

Knowing the various types of Psalms can help us identify their structure and often their purpose. It is less certain whether the "life setting" (German: *Sitz-em-Leben* "situation in life") or the original historical background of the psalm can be determined, as classical Old Testament form criticism attempts to do. Form criticism can be useful in the Pentateuch by noting the similarities to various ancient Near

Eastern law codes and treaty structures (e.g., it is generally accepted that Deuteronomy follows the form of a Hittite suzerain-vassal treaty).

Rhetorical Criticism: Rhetorical criticism examines how a literary unit is put together to achieve its purpose: How does the prophet build his argument for the greatest effect? How does the narrator craft the story to focus attention on the main point? How does the psalmist develop the emotion of the psalm and for what purpose? This is similar to examining a play and trying to determine how each of the scenes are developed and what things were included to get across the message of the play, like how the author used dialogue to advance the message, or how a court scene helped develop the theme. James Muilenburg identifies the difference between form criticism and rhetorical criticism by claiming that the former tends to generalize and deals with forms that are typical and representative of a genre, while the latter deals primarily with the unique and personal characteristics of the author.[5]

Given Muilenburg's position, rhetorical techniques include figures of speech (e.g., simile, metaphor), literary or compositional techniques (e.g., parallel structure, chiasm, rhetorical questions), and an examination of the relationship of a passage's form to its meaning. Thus, even diversities that occur in the typical forms are important and should cause the exegete to question their underlying purpose. For example, Psalm 40 contains a very unusual structure for a psalm since it appears to contain both the elements of a thanksgiving psalm in vv. 1–10 and an individual lament psalm in vv. 11–17. This is one of the few psalms (if not the only one) that ends with the psalmist still in need—without either God having already delivered him or at least a statement of trust that God soon will deliver him. Scholars commonly suggest that this psalm is a combination of two psalms or that something has been lost. Since the last part of Psalm 40 is almost exactly the same as Psalm 70, maybe it is possible that the psalmist is applying this latter psalm to his current situation. Or maybe the psalmist is confident that God will indeed deliver him based upon past experience—since God has done it in the past—thus He will do it in the current situation. Either way

---

5. James Muilenburg, "Form Criticism and Beyond," *JBL* 88 (March 1969): 5.

the structure of this psalm is extremely interesting and must cause the exegete to ask important questions regarding its arrangement.

Questions are another important rhetorical device, such as that found in Psalm 2:1: "Why are the nations in tumult or the peoples uttering empty things?" The next verses describe these empty words and senseless attempts to overthrow God and His king.

Redaction Criticism: Redaction criticism is interested in the overall assemblage of a text and what it communicates about the editor's (redactor's) perspective or meaning. Some more recent scholars have suggested that an editor or redactor has taken what the original biblical author has said and significantly reshaped it. This would be like a modern editor going over an author's work and either clarifying it (i.e., making it say more clearly what the author intended) or modifying it to mean something that the original author did not intend. While the books of Chronicles contain material that is parallel to that of Samuel and Kings, they clearly demonstrate a different purpose than the earlier books. Whoever did the shaping and editing of the books of Chronicles provides encouragement for the post-exilic community by highlighting God's gracious actions throughout Israel's history—God was not finished with them and they needed to know that. While the book of 2 Kings ends with Jehoiachin living out his days in Babylon, the book of 2 Chronicles ends with Cyrus, the king of Persia, allowing the Israelites to return to Israel and rebuild Yahweh's temple. The narratives which were both selected and omitted reflect the editor's intention to encourage the people with God's faithfulness.

2. Immediate Context

The immediate context of a text deals with specific verses or paragraphs and requires questions like: What is the original reading of the text? What are the proper meanings of the words in this context? How do the phrases relate to each other? What does each sentence add to the argument or development of the paragraph? Forms of literary analysis dealing primarily with the immediate context and which prove extremely helpful in Old Testament exegesis include textual criticism, lexical analysis, and syntactical analysis.

Textual Criticism: Textual criticism is the examination of known sources of an Old Testament passage in order to reconstruct the original wording of the biblical text. This is not always possible due to a lack of evidence, but for the most part the Hebrew text of the Old Testament appears to be very accurate. This is extremely important for pastors, for unless we have a good biblical text to begin with, no matter how much we study for our sermons, they will still be flawed. The apparatus in *BHS* provides valuable textual evidence for difficult passages in the Hebrew text; however, it assumes a thorough knowledge of Hebrew and much of it is written in Latin abbreviations. English Bibles often note difficult or uncertain readings in the Old Testament but provide little information beyond that. Without more information it can be difficult to know the exact problem, and the notes do not generally supply a solution. As a result, laypersons may question the accuracy of the text. Unless the difficulty is resolved, it will only cause fear and frustration. For example, the footnote in the English Standard Version for Psalm 145:13 says, "These two lines are supplied by one Hebrew manuscript, Septuagint, Syriac (compare Dead Sea Scroll)." This would cause most people to wonder why the lines are missing and had to be supplied. Is their Bible faulty? Is it loaded with errors in other places also? In actual fact, there are a few places in the Old Testament where variants make some difference in the meaning of the text and this is one of them. Psalm 145 is an alphabetic acrostic in which the *nûn* verse appears to be missing from the Hebrew text. The textual apparatus for *BHS* suggests inserting the following verse into the Hebrew text:

נֶאֱמָן יהוה בְּכָל־דְּבָרָיו ׀ וְחָסִיד בְּכָל־מַעֲשָׂיו

"The LORD is faithful in all his words
and kind in all his deeds."

This reading is found in one Hebrew manuscript, the Septuagint, and the Syriac Peshitta and is quite similar to verse 17. It appears that this verse fell out of the Hebrew text sometime after the translation of the Septuagint. It would be highly unlikely for an alphabetic acrostic not to contain a *nûn* verse, thus I believe it should be included in the Hebrew text.

Lexical Analysis: Just as English dictionaries provide specific meanings of words, so biblical Hebrew dictionaries or lexicons provide meanings for Hebrew words. It is possible that a word may have a different meaning or nuance depending upon the context or type of literature. Sometimes knowing the specific meaning of a Hebrew word will provide the key to understand the passage. For example the Hebrew word טוֹב *ṭôb* "good" has a range of meanings from "morally good" or "pleasing" (Hos. 8:3) to "suitable" and "fitting" (1 Kings 2:38). In Isaiah 39:8, after Hezekiah shows the emissaries from Babylon all that he has, Isaiah tells Hezekiah that all his possessions will be carried off to Babylon. In response Hezekiah says, "'The word of the LORD which you have spoken is good.' For he thought, there will be peace and truth in my days." This response makes Hezekiah look like a jerk who only cares about himself. However, if we realize that טוֹב *ṭôb* should probably be translated as "suitable" or "fitting," his reaction makes more sense. It would send the wrong message if God allowed the Babylonians to destroy Judah during the reign of one of the most godly kings in Israel's history. Therefore Hezekiah's response that it is "suitable" or "fitting" for God to allow the deportation after his reign is reasonable.

Several of the works mentioned in the previous chapter will provide the busy pastor or student with in-depth lexical analyses of important Hebrew words. One area of significant improvement in modern Hebrew dictionaries is the realization of the importance of context over etymologies in determining a word's meaning—something that James Barr pointed out more than forty-five years ago.[6] See appendix C for a guide on how to conduct a complete Hebrew word study. However, an entire word study is often unnecessary—even a fairly superficial examination of the usage of important words often uncovers important gems for a sermon. For example, most English translations of 1 Samuel 15:3 read "strike Amalek and *utterly destroy* all that is his," or something quite similar. But the text uses the verbal root חרם (*ḥrm*) which suggests that the Amalekites were to be set apart and given over to God. It is related to the noun *ḥerem*, which commonly refers to women set apart and given

---

6. James Barr, *The Semantics of Biblical Language* (Oxford: Oxford University Press, 1961), 412–36.

over to a king. It is the word used when referring to the destruction of Jericho, for it was to be totally destroyed and set apart for God. Thus Saul's refusal to set apart or dedicate everything to God suggests that Saul may not have felt God was worth the best things, but merely the despised and worthless ones.

Understanding specific meanings of the words is a good start to understanding a passage, but it is just the beginning. The next step is a syntactical analysis.

Syntactical Analysis: A syntactical analysis is probably the most useful tool for determining the meaning of a passage. It involves diagramming the flow of the passage and indicates how the phrases relate to one another. Referring back to the Hebrew text is often a necessity since English translations may allow for several interpretations of a passage. For example, in Isaiah 9:2–5 (English vv. 3–6) there is a clear syntactical relationship that is easily overlooked in English translations. Verse 2 (English v. 3) speaks of God's multiplying the nation and bringing great joy which the author likens to the joy of harvest and of dividing up spoil after a great victory. The next three verses go on to give three major reasons for this great joy. Each of these verses begins with the Hebrew word כִּי "for" to introduce a reason for this joy. First, they will be released from their subjugation; second, the battle garments will be burned up (suggesting a time of peace during which they are no longer needed); and third, a ruler will be born who will usher in a time of peace, righteousness, and justice.

Syntactical analysis of a Hebrew passage is often less complicated than Greek. Generally it is best not to break a Hebrew sentence down further than phrases or clauses so as not to lose the flow of the passage. Prepositions and even particles are very important in determining how phrases are related. See appendices D and E for a detailed explanation on how to do a syntactical analysis of a passage.

Historical Analysis

Historical analysis deals primarily with background matters such as author, date, historical context, audience, purpose, customs, and cultural and sociological backgrounds. It is a somewhat artificial distinction because other components of literary and theological analysis are clearly dependent on the history and culture, but it is nonetheless worth addressing separately. In historical analysis, you want to ask about the geography of the text and the significance of it (e.g., does the story concern the northern kingdom or the southern kingdom?). You also want to investigate the ancient Near Eastern situation at the time; the history of God's people is intertwined with the power struggles between international empires. Additionally, investigate whether there have been any relevant archaeological findings that shed light on your passage. Be certain as well to find any other biblical passages that shed light on the setting of your text (e.g., a study of Kings must also include the prophetic books that are parallel with the historical events).

Historical analysis has been more widely abused among preachers than any other area of analysis, not only because the Old Testament is describing events and situations several thousand years removed from us, but also because we do not understand many of the customs and historical events within the text. Customs like polygamy, covenant enactment ceremonies, birthrights, and many others are foreign to modern Western culture and erect many interpretational barriers for today's readers. Thus pastors have the dual challenge of understanding ancient Near Eastern culture and explaining these ancient customs in a way that makes sense. Research and study is crucial to this process.

A good example of the importance of understanding ancient Near Eastern culture is found in Genesis 15 when Abraham asks God how he will know that God will fulfill His promises. God answers by making a covenant with Abraham. Covenants were the strongest assurance in the ancient Near East that people would keep their promises. In a covenant, a person called upon the gods to bring curses on the one who did not follow through with the covenant. In the situation with Abraham, God swears that if He does not keep His promises, He will cut Himself in half like the animal carcasses. When God holds Himself to such a high standard of commitment, Abraham can rest assured that God's promises will come to pass.

Theological Analysis

Theological analysis examines what the Bible says about God, His nature, His relationship to creation, and other such issues, and then it determines a text's meaning for today's congregations. The field of studies known as canonical criticism finds its home here. Canonical criticism looks at the largest context of a passage—the entire Bible—and asks about the theological significance of a particular text "within the community of faith that preserved and treasured them."[7] In its broadest application, canonical criticism asks about the significance of a text for *contemporary* communities of faith.

Each biblical book was written for a purpose and provides revelation that integrates into the overall message of the Bible, thus the exegete must ask broad questions: How does a book or passage incorporate into the rest of Scripture? What was the purpose for the final form of the biblical text? What information is gained by reading each book within the parameters of the canon of Scripture? What does this passage add to the overall message of Scripture and what is its purpose? What material is unique to each book and why is it important? Probably one of the most important issues when reading the Old Testament within its canonical context or even for developing our theology is how some Old Testament passages are picked up and reused in the New Testament to refer to Jesus, the Messiah. The New Testament book of Matthew is known for applying Old Testament passages to Jesus (e.g., Isa. 7:14; Micah 5:2; Hosea 11:1), but sometimes it is difficult to see how they apply. A very clear example is found in Matthew 2:15 where the author states that Hosea 11:1 has been fulfilled by Jesus coming out of Egypt. But Hosea 11:1 very clearly states, "When Israel was a lad I loved him and from Egypt I called my son." There is no doubt that the passage is referring to Israel being called out of Egypt, not Jesus; so how can Matthew say this? I believe that we have misunderstood what Matthew meant by "fulfilled" and have understood it to mean a direct fulfillment of that passage—which is sometimes how New Testament authors use this word (see John 18:9, 32). However, when Matthew uses it, it appears to mean "to fill up (with meaning)," a legitimate usage of the Greek word. Thus Matthew is showing his readers how Jesus "fills up" a passage even further, adding more meaning to some of the Old Testament passages. Whenever we preach Old Testament passages, I believe it is important to show how the New Testament picks them up

---

7. Richard N. Soulen, *Handbook of Biblical Criticism*, 2nd ed. (Atlanta: John Knox, 1981), 37.

and uses them—sometimes applying them directly to Christ, sometimes allowing Jesus to fill them up even further.

Another critical element of theological analysis is what is commonly called "progressive revelation." The concept is that God revealed material to His people over a long period in the Old Testament and this should affect how we interpret Scripture. Each time God revealed something new, it became His authoritative message which He expected to be obeyed. Probably the best way to understand the relationship between the Old and New Testaments is that the Old Testament prepares a firm foundation for the New Testament, with concepts like sacrifice, circumcision, Passover, and the law, which take on even further significance in the New Testament. It is tempting to want to read material that is revealed later into earlier passages, but this is anachronistic and can lead to incorrect interpretations. A good example can be found in Genesis 4 where Cain and Abel both bring an offering to the Lord. It says that God had regard for Abel and his offering, but not for Cain and his offering. It is tempting to explain the reason for God not being pleased with Cain and his offering was because it was not a blood sacrifice, which later we learn is a fitting sacrifice for a sin offering. However, this is unlikely in this passage for two reasons: (1) As far as we can tell, God had not yet revealed the importance of blood sacrifices as sin offerings (see Lev. 5:9; 8:15; 17:11); and (2) the Hebrew word מִנְחָה (minḥâ "gift, offering") is commonly used for a gift of grain (e.g., Exod. 29:41; 30:9; Lev. 2:1, 3–5; Num. 6:17). In Genesis 4 it is more likely that God was not pleased with Cain's offering because of his attitude, as suggested in the New Testament (Heb. 11:4; 1 John 3:12).

One of the most important theological concepts in the Old Testament is the New Covenant referred to in Jeremiah 31:31–34. Using theological analysis to trace this idea through Scripture yields rich results. The passage in Jeremiah states three new outcomes from the New Covenant: (1) "I will write My law within them" is fulfilled in Acts 2 when God sends the Holy Spirit to live in believers' hearts (see the promised coming of the Spirit in John 14:16–17); (2) "they will all know Me from the least of them to the greatest" is fulfilled in the New Testament in that believers can come directly to God without needing a human priest as intermediary (Christ fulfils that role, Heb. 7); and (3) "for I will forgive their iniquity and their sin I will remember no longer" is fulfilled in Christ's work on the cross—in the Old Testament sins were covered by the blood of a sacrifice, but in the New Testament our sins are obliterated by the shed blood of Christ. Jesus even confirms that the Lord's Supper (or communion) is a reminder of the New Covenant and the blood that Jesus shed to inaugurate this covenant (Matt. 26:26–29; Mark 14:22–25; Luke 22:14–20).

APPLICATION

The Old Testament text is several thousand years old, so how does a pastor apply it today? This is probably the most important part of the exegetical sermon, for unless the content of the Word of God is made applicable to the person, it will soon be forgotten. Exegeting a passage is not complete until we have underscored its relevance and application to today, and helped our listeners understand what God is saying well enough to integrate it into their own lives. It is knowledge that should prompt change—either in attitude or action. I have found that the better you understand the passage, the easier it is to make clear and specific points of application. So how do you make those points of application?

The historical situations and the temporal elements of the story may change, but the timeless principles embedded in Scripture remain true. For example, principles in the story of David and Goliath include (1) we need not fear God's enemies when we are fighting for Him; (2) there will always be something that looks impossible, but we can conquer it with God's help; and (3) those who mock our God will not go unpunished. These principles are specific to a point, but there is still the need to illustrate what they look like when in action today. For instance, we can show how the passage addresses situations such as: "I just lost my job. Can I trust God to get me through this?" "I just witnessed to my friend and he laughed at me. Should I just give up witnessing?" "I feel over-worked, unloved, and tired. Can God help me?" David Alan Black states it this way: "Preachers do not *make* the text relevant; they should get deep enough into the text to *find* its relevance."[8]

Scripture records historical events and past actions

---

8. David Alan Black, *Using New Testament Greek in Ministry: A Practical Guide for Students and Pastors* (Grand Rapids: Baker, 1993), 86.

of God to teach us about God's changeless character. He will act in the same way today. What will it take to make the people in your church believe that the same God that brought down the walls of Jericho (Josh. 6), or made hailstones fall from heaven (Josh. 10:11), or stopped the sun in the middle of the sky (Josh. 10:12–14), still loves and cares for them? Isaiah may have said it best: "The grass withers, the flower fades, but the word of our God stands forever" (Isa. 40:8).

If understood properly, the biblical text will change you as much as it will change the lives of the people in your congregation. As you learn new ways to love and serve God, you can share those ideas with your congregation and help them grow. A pastor needs to dig deeply into the biblical text so that he can lead his congregation into those depths. Scripture becomes a well that energizes both pastor and congregation. Sheep only follow a shepherd as far as the shepherd can lead them, and your love and depth of understanding of Scripture will either exhilarate your congregation, or they will grow bored with its shallowness.

CONCLUSION

The work of an exegete is a rigorous journey that takes time and effort to do well, but pays great dividends in our lives and those of our congregations. The Holy Spirit uses clear explanations of God's Word to gradually mold listeners into more godly people. Very few things are more important for a pastor or student of the Bible than to learn how to mine the riches of Scripture for themselves and for others. Each step of literary analysis, historical analysis, and theological analysis will take you deeper into the biblical text and will provide the jewels that can then be applied to people's lives. Take the time and effort to mine the gold and it will pay rich dividends.

THINGS TO CONSIDER

Some of the issues raised in this chapter are crucial to ministry and require careful thought:

1. Are you willing to work hard to make sure your congregation will be constantly fed, even though you may not see much immediate fruit?

2. Does discovering new things in God's Word motivate you to dig deeper, in hopes of being able to share those things with others?

3. Can you make biblical exegesis a priority, and do you see the necessity of expounding God's Word to a congregation?

4. Are there things you may have to give up or pass on to someone else to make biblical exegesis a priority?

FURTHER READING

Chisholm, Robert B., Jr. *From Exegesis to Exposition: A Practical Guide to Using Biblical Hebrew.* Grand Rapids: Baker, 1998.

Kaiser, Walter C. *Preaching and Teaching from the Old Testament: A Guide for the Church.* Grand Rapids: Baker, 2003. See especially pages 58–59, 173–204.

Klein, William W. Craig L. Blomberg, and Robert L. Hubbard, Jr. *Introduction to Biblical Interpretation.* Dallas: Word, 1993.

Larson, David L. "Preaching the Old Testament Today." Pages 171–83 in *Preaching the Old Testament.* Edited by Scott M. Gibson. Grand Rapids: Baker, 2006.

MacDonald, James, Lyle Dorsett, John Beukema, John Koessler, and Steve Nicholson. "Sermon Application in a Post-Christian Culture (Parts 1–3): Applying God's Truth Where Biblical Authority Is Questioned," http://www.preachingtoday.com/16868 (accessed January 5, 2007).

Osborne, Grant R. *The Hermeneutical Spiral: A Comprehensive Introduction to Biblical Interpretation.* Revised edition. Downers Grove, IL: InterVarsity Press, 2006.

Robinson, Haddon W. *Biblical Preaching: The Development and Delivery of Expository Messages.* 2nd ed. Grand Rapids: Baker, 2001.

CHAPTER
FOUR

DEVELOPING A PRACTICAL PLAN

HOW DO I PREPARE AN OLD TESTAMENT SERMON?

*The Levites explained the law to the people while the
people remained in their place. They read from the
book, from the law of God, translating to give the
sense so that they understood the reading.*
—Nehemiah 8:7–8

The previous three chapters have laid the groundwork so that now we can make a practical plan for developing a sermon from the Hebrew text. This is where the fun really begins because this plan will not only help us prepare sermons, it will also enrich our own Bible study. Bridging the historical/cultural gap between the Old Testament text and today's readers is not easy—it can be significantly more complicated to apply than the New Testament. For this reason, we will spend more time here explaining how to do just that.

Where do we start? The following eleven steps provide the basics of Old Testament exegesis, from examining the historical setting and background of the text to developing a sermon from it. The process assumes you have a basic proficiency in translating the Hebrew text (at the beginning proficiency may be fairly minimal, but in time this will improve),

87

hermeneutics, historical and cultural backgrounds of the Old Testament, and homiletics. This process will bring together all that you have learned or will learn in seminary or Bible school and help you focus on specific Old Testament passages. Expect to spend about twenty hours developing a full exegetical sermon with the right illustrations to drive the points home.

Here is a brief description of the steps, spelled out in the acrostic "READ THE BOOK."

BRIEF DESCRIPTION OF OLD TESTAMENT EXEGESIS	
R–Read the book.	Read the entire biblical book two or three times in English to get the big picture.
E–Establish a good translation of the passage.	Translate the section of Hebrew text you will be expounding and compare other English translations.
A–Ascertain the original reading of the text.	Before examining the passage in detail, determine the original wording. If there are major textual issues, modern translations will most likely have a brief footnote of explanation. Generally it is not necessary to highlight this information in a sermon, but it will be important for you to have a good understanding of what you believe to be the original text.
D–Determine the historical setting.	To understand and apply the passage as it was originally intended, it is necessary to know its original historical setting.
T–Take note of the literary structure.	It is crucial to understand how the passage fits into the context of the whole book. What is its purpose and why did the author write it? Determine the flow of thought, the author's argument, and the literary genre.
H–Highlight the meanings of words (word studies).	Some words are essential for a proper understanding of the passage. Word studies will uncover important nuances in the meaning(s) of the words.

E–Examine the syntax and grammar.	A syntactical analysis is an important tool for understanding the meaning of the text. Especially take note of any syntactical issues that help determine or clarify the meaning of the text.
B–Begin building the sermon.	Develop an outline from the results of your exegesis and use the main points of your outline to build the core of your sermon. Select a key word that links the points together (e.g., reasons, steps, conclusions, arguments) and then make the main points as relevant to your audience as possible.
O–Observe theological issues.	What does this passage add to God's revelation? What new things have you learned about God or how He wants us to behave? How does it fit with other passages dealing with the same theological issues?
O–Offer clear illustrations and application.	How do I illustrate and help make the text applicable to people's lives? Illustrations help people see how a truth might relate to their present situations. Application helps people put that truth to use in their lives. Applying the text so that it meets the needs of listeners is one of the most important considerations.
K–Keep prayer a priority.	Prayer is often overlooked, but it is only through God's power flowing through your words that lives will be changed.

These eleven steps will ensure you have been thorough in your preparation to expound God's Word. Exegeting the Hebrew text is not easy, but it is worth it. Nothing else can provide such depth to your preaching. The last step, prayer, is also an essential part of the preparation—don't shortchange it. George Müller reminds us:

> It is a common temptation of Satan to make us give up the reading of the Word and prayer when our enjoyment is gone; as if it were of no use to read the Scriptures when we do not enjoy them,

and as if it were no use to pray when we have no spirit of prayer; the truth is, whilst in order to enjoy the Word, we ought to continue to read it, and the way to obtain a spirit of prayer, is to continue praying; for the less we read the Word of God, the less we desire to read it, and the less we pray, the less we desire to pray.[1]

As we look at the steps in more detail, remember that they are intended as a guide to direct your exegesis. Some steps will not be as useful as others in certain passages, so tailor the process to fit your needs. You can also modify the process to make it your own—you may want to add steps, move them around, or even remove parts. Included in the discussion of each step is a bibliography in case you should desire to dig more deeply.

THE DETAILS OF EACH STEP

1. Read the Book

Since the Old Testament is still foreign ground to most pastors and students, it is all the more necessary to become very familiar with the book you are preaching. Begin with a broad look at the book or section you are analyzing by reading it through in its entirety, and then narrow down to the specific passage. Examining a few verses without knowing how they integrate into the book as a whole is like focusing on one puzzle piece without seeing the bigger picture. John G. Mitchell, one of the founders of Multnomah School of the Bible, went to hear G. Campbell Morgan preach. Young Mitchell was very impressed at how well the older preacher knew the text. He went up afterward to ask Morgan how he had gained his knowledge of Scripture. "If I told you, you wouldn't do it," the older man said. "Just try me," Mitchell insisted. "Before I study a book, I read it fifty times," the veteran explained.[2] What an excellent way to allow the biblical text to infiltrate your life.

After you have read the entire book through several times,

---

1. George Müller, *A Narrative of Some of the Lord's Dealings with George Müller* (Muskegon, MI: Dust & Ashes Publications, 2003), 1:44.
2. Sermon Illustrations, "Bible, study of," http://www.sermonillustrations .com/a-z/b/bible_study_of.htm (accessed August 12, 2006).

you will begin to see its flow of thought and main sections. If you are going to preach or teach a series on a particular book, then decide how much of the book you want to cover in each sermon and determine your sermon themes. This is an essential part of good sermon preparation. Covering too many verses may overwhelm listeners and force you to merely skim the surface. Going too slowly may cause even the most patient congregation to lose interest. If necessary, pick the most important passages to preach on and simply summarize other sections. Look for natural breaks in the book and avoid splitting up sections that should be together. Chapter divisions do not always reflect natural breaks in thought (for example, Isa. 4:1 is clearly part of the curses at the end of chapter 3), so carefully analyze the passage to make sure it is a self-contained unit. The process of dividing up the book into preaching passages will provide a useful guide for you and the congregation to understand the structure of the book.

Prepare this preaching structure well in advance so that you can work ahead. Dividing up your week will also help you stay on track with your exegesis. I suggest dedicating two mornings a week to reading a biblical book, familiarizing yourself with its historical background, and translating the passage to be preached. Two additional mornings can be set aside for actual sermon preparation. There will always be urgent pastoral matters such as illnesses or deaths that take time during the week, but if you are working ahead emergencies will have less effect on your sermon preparation. Preaching a series on a book or part of a book also saves valuable preparation time since the historical background information will only need to be gathered once.

Helpful Resources

Adler, Mortimer J., and Charles Van Doren. *How to Read a Book*. New York: Simon and Schuster, 1940. Many later editions are available as well.

Dewey, David. *A User's Guide to Bible Translations: Making the Most of Different Versions*. Downers Grove, IL: InterVarsity Press, 2005.

Fee, Gordon D., and Douglas K. Stuart. *How to Read the Bible for All Its Worth*. 3rd ed. Grand Rapids: Zondervan, 2003.

Fee, Gordon D., and Mark L. Strauss. *How to Choose a Translation for All Its Worth: A Guide to Understanding and Using Bible Versions.* Grand Rapids: Zondervan, 2007.

Online source: The American Bible Society has a good overview to help you determine which Bible translation is best for you (http://www.americanbible.org/brcpages/bibletranslation).

2. Establish a Good Translation of the Passage

Translate the passage you are preaching. Look up key words and choose the most accurate nuances of words in this section of Scripture. Use Hebrew grammars and syntax books (e.g., Williams, or Waltke and O'Connor) to discover nuances of verb stems and how prepositions are used, and check Hebrew lexicons for specific meanings of words. If you are not sure of the parsing, use a computer program or parsing guide (e.g., Beall, Banks, and Smith). Remember that a single Hebrew word rarely overlaps perfectly with the range of meanings of a single English word. Sometimes using several English words or a phrase may help express the Hebrew meaning more fully. Although this type of detailed translation is time consuming, it is the best way to make sure your sermon's foundation is solid. Computer programs may speed up your work here to save time.

Check your translation against a literal word-for-word translation (e.g., RSV, NASBU, ESV). Unlike modern translations, you do not have to be overly concerned with wordiness or readability. Your goal should be accuracy even if it produces a long translation or awkward phrasing. Because modern English translations are typically the result of careful work by a group of scholars, it can be valuable to compare a number of translations to see where they differ. This may also highlight textual difficulties in the Hebrew text. At times it may be useful to note important differences between translations in a sermon, especially if the congregation uses a variety of Bible translations or if specific translations pose significant problems.

If you get behind in your translating or if you have a very long passage, then only translate key sections. Leave the rest for later if you come back to the book or passage. At the very least check a literal word-for-word translation against the Hebrew text to see if you agree and are satisfied with its translation. It will take less time to check a translation than create a new one and you can at least obtain a sense of how accurately it reflects the original text.

Helpful Resources

GRAMMARS OR SYNTAX BOOKS

Kautzsch, E. *Gesenius' Hebrew Grammar.* Translated by A. E. Cowley. 2nd ed. Oxford: Oxford University Press, 1910. Especially the biblical passage index.

Waltke, Bruce K., and M. O'Connor. *An Introduction to Biblical Hebrew Syntax.* Winona Lake, IN: Eisenbrauns, 1990. Especially the biblical passage index.

Williams, Ronald J. *Williams' Hebrew Syntax.* Revised and expanded by John C. Beckman. 3rd ed. Toronto: University of Toronto Press, 2007. Especially the Hebrew prepositions and particles on the last couple of pages of the book.

HEBREW LEXICONS AND PARSING GUIDES

Beall, Todd S., William A. Banks, and Colin Smith. *Old Testament Parsing Guide.* Revised and updated edition. Nashville: Broadman and Holman, 2000.

Brown, Francis, S. R. Driver, and C. A. Briggs. *Hebrew and English Lexicon of the Old Testament.* Oxford: Clarendon, 1906. Corrected by G. R. Driver, Oxford: Clarendon, 1951. Reprint, Peabody, MA: Hendrickson, 1998.

Davidson, Benjamin. *Analytical Hebrew-Chaldee Lexicon.* 1848. Reprint, Peabody, MA: Hendrickson, 1981.

Koehler, L., W. Baumgartner, and J. J. Stamm. *The Hebrew and Aramaic Lexicon of the Old Testament* [*HALOT*]. Translated and edited under the supervision of M. E. J. Richardson. 5 vols. Leiden: Brill, 1994–2000.

LITERAL TRANSLATIONS OF THE BIBLE

English Standard Version
New American Standard Bible
New King James Version
New Revised Standard Version
Revised Standard Version

OTHER POPULAR TRANSLATIONS AND PARAPHRASES

Holman Christian Standard Bible
New Living Translation

New International Version
The Good News Bible
The Message
Today's New International Version

3. Ascertain the Original Reading of the Text
    As noted above, questions about the original reading
of the Hebrew text may surface when you compare several English translations. The best place to start sorting
out these questions is the critical apparatus of *BHS*–it will
provide much of the evidence necessary for this investiga-
tion. The apparatus includes other forms of the Hebrew text
(e.g., Qumran manuscripts, medieval manuscripts of the
Masoretic Text [MT]), as well as other ancient versions (e.g.,
Septuagint, Samaritan Pentateuch, Syriac Peshitta, Latin
Vulgate). However, the information in this apparatus often
can be difficult to use since: (1) the editors assume an advanced knowledge of the Hebrew language, (2) there are
numerous Latin abbreviations, and (3) words from other ancient versions are not translated. Nevertheless, with English
translations, biblical commentaries, and English translations of the ancient versions, this study can be readily
undertaken.
    Sometimes it is apparent that a copying mistake, or a
misunderstanding of the Hebrew vowel pointing or grammar
gave rise to a variant. In more complicated cases, use critical commentaries that discuss the textual variants. In general, only about 10 percent of the MT poses any questions
regarding the original reading, and of these, only a small
portion significantly affect the meaning. When in doubt, it is
advisable to retain the MT and just make a note concerning
the difficulties of the passage.
    A good example of how Old Testament textual criticism
makes a significant difference in the reading of a passage
can be found in Genesis 4:8 which literally reads "and Cain
said to Abel his brother, and it came about when they were
in the field, . . ." There appears to be an omission of what
Cain said to Abel. The textual apparatus for *BHS* suggests
inserting the following phrase into the Hebrew text:

$$\text{נֵלְכָה הַשָּׂדֶה}$$

"Let us go (to) the field."

This phrase is found in the Samaritan Pentateuch, the Septuagint, the Syriac Peshitta, and the Latin Vulgate; some Hebrew manuscripts contain a space here. It appears that this phrase fell out of the Hebrew text sometime after the translation of the Septuagint, possibly confusing similar letters. Specifically, the Hebrew word "his brother" ends with *yôd, wāw* and the next word begins with *wāw, yôd*. This combination of letters may have caused the scribe to skip to the second (*wāw, yôd*), leaving out material in between.

Helpful Resources

Good Overviews

Tov, Emanuel. "Textual Criticism (OT)." Pages 393–412 in vol. 6 of *Anchor Bible Dictionary*. Edited by D. N. Freedman. 6 vols. New York: Doubleday, 1992.

Waltke, Bruce K. "The Textual Criticism of the Old Testament." Pages 211–28 in vol. 1 of *Expositor's Bible Commentary*. Edited by F. E. Gaebelein. 12 vols. Grand Rapids: Zondervan, 1979.

Critical Hebrew Editions

Althann, R., et al., eds. *Biblia Hebraica Quinta*. 5th ed. Stuttgart: Deutsche Bibelgesellschaft, 2004–.

Elliger, K., and W. Rudolph, eds. *Biblia Hebraica Stuttgartensia*. 4th ed. Stuttgart: Deutsche Bibelgesellschaft, 1967–77.

Textual Critical Helps

Critical commentaries on the Hebrew text (often in the "notes" section or footnotes on the translation)

Hatch, Edwin, and Henry A. Redpath. *Concordance to the Septuagint and Other Greek Versions of the Old Testament*. 3 vols. Oxford: Clarendon, 1897–1906. Reprint, Grand Rapids: Baker, 1998.

Kelley, Page H., Daniel S. Mynatt, and Timothy G. Crawford. *The Masorah of Biblia Hebraica Stuttgartensia: Introduction and Annotated Glossary*. Grand Rapids: Eerdmans, 1998.

Scott, William R. *A Simplified Guide to BHS: Critical Apparatus, Masora, Accents, Unusual Letters and Other Markings*. 3rd ed. Berkeley: BIBAL, 1995.

Tov, Emanuel. *Textual Criticism of the Hebrew Bible*. 2nd ed. Minneapolis: Fortress; Assen: Van Gorcum, 2001.

Wegner, Paul D. *A Student's Guide to Textual Criticism of the Bible: Its History, Methods and Results.* Downers Grove, IL: InterVarsity Press, 2006.

Wonneberger, Reinhard. *Understanding BHS: A Manual for the Users of* Biblia Hebraica. Translated by Dwight R. Daniels. 3rd ed. Stuttgartensia: Jesuit Consortium, 2001.

4. Determine the Historical Setting

Knowing the historical context and setting of a passage can be crucial to understanding what the author is saying. Ignoring them can easily lead to misinterpretation. One of the most basic hermeneutical principles is to determine the message the biblical author or editor intended to convey to his original audience. Study Bibles, Bible dictionaries or encyclopedias, Bible handbooks, and good commentaries can provide this information. A historical analysis looks at the author, date, audience, occasion, purpose, culture, and geography. It tries to answer the who, what, when, where, and why of a passage. The following is a sample of questions to ask:

1. Where does our passage fit in God's progressive revelation to His people?

2. Why is the author writing this section and to whom?

3. What are the specific situations that gave rise to the passage?

4. What is happening historically and socially, and how does it impact the passage?

5. Are there cultural or geographical issues that factor into the passage?

This information can often be used in the introduction to your series or in individual sermons. Most likely it will be new to many listeners and can add insights when they read the passage later. Old Testament material is often written against a backdrop of unbelief or disobedience to God. If you can determine why the author or prophet says what he does, it can bring the passage to life and often be applied in a similar fashion to today's situations. For instance, the historical and cultural setting of the book of Jonah is essential to understanding the dynamics of the story. Jonah does not want to warn the Ninevites that God is about to destroy them. In chapter 4 he gives the reason: he knows that God is gracious and compassionate and "relents concerning calamity." In other words, Jonah does not want God to be gracious to the Ninevites and "let them off." God can be gracious to him and other Israelites, but not to the pagan Assyrians. He doesn't want to share his God—let the Assyrian gods protect them. The point of the story is that Jonah needs to learn that God is not only Israel's God, but the God of the whole world. God shows Jonah that He loves everyone and can show mercy to anyone. This becomes a hard pill to swallow for the Israelites, who are cruelly treated by the Assyrians as history unfolds. What a tremendous message to us today—do we really believe that God loves everyone or do we try to keep Him all to ourselves?

Helpful Resources

BOOKS ON ISRAEL'S HISTORY

COMMENTARIES (IN THE INTRODUCTION ON HISTORY/SETTING)

Bright, John. *A History of Israel.* 4th ed. Louisville: Westminster John Knox, 2000.

Kaiser, Walter C. *A History of Israel: From the Bronze Age to the Jewish Wars.* Nashville: Broadman and Holman, 1998.

Merrill, Eugene H. *A Kingdom of Priests: A History of Old Testament Israel.* 2nd ed. Grand Rapids: Baker, 2008.

Miller, J. Maxwell, and John H. Hayes. *A History of Ancient Israel and Judah.* 2nd ed. Louisville: Westminster John Knox, 2006.

CUSTOMS/GEOGRAPHY

Aharoni, Yohanan, Michael Avi-Yonah, Anson F. Rainey, and Ze'ev Safrai. *The Macmillan Bible Atlas.* 3rd ed. New York: Macmillan, 1993. This work is now called *The Carta Bible Atlas.* 4th ed. Jerusalem: Carta, 2002.

Beitzel, Barry J. *The Moody Atlas of Bible Lands.* Chicago: Moody, 1985.

Rasmussen, Carl G. *Zondervan NIV Atlas of the Bible.* Grand Rapids: Zondervan, 1999.

Walton, John H., Victor H. Matthews, and Mark W. Chavalas. *The IVP Bible Background Commentary: Old Testament.* Downers Grove, IL: InterVarsity Press, 2000.

GENERAL DICTIONARIES/ENCYCLOPEDIAS/HANDBOOKS/
OLD TESTAMENT INTRODUCTIONS/OLD TESTAMENT SURVEYS

Arnold, Bill T., and Bryan E. Beyer. *Encountering the Old Testament: A Christian Survey.* 2nd ed. Grand Rapids: Baker, 2008.

Bromiley, Geoffrey W., ed. *The International Standard Bible Encyclopedia.* Revised edition. 4 vols. Grand Rapids: Eerdmans, 1979.

Douglas, James D., and N. Hillyer, eds. *The Illustrated Bible Dictionary.* 3 vols. Wheaton, IL: Tyndale House, 1980.

Freedman, David N., ed. *Anchor Bible Dictionary.* 6 vols. New York: Doubleday, 1992.

Harrison, Roland K. *Introduction to the Old Testament.* Grand Rapids: Eerdmans, 1969.

Hill, Andrew E., and John H. Walton. *A Survey of the Old Testament.* 2nd ed. Grand Rapids: Zondervan, 2000.

LaSor, William S., David A. Hubbard, and Frederic W. Bush. *Old Testament Survey: The Message, Form, and Background of the Old Testament.* 2nd ed. Grand Rapids: Eerdmans, 1996.

5. Take Note of the Literary Structure

Analyzing the literary context of an Old Testament passage may add further clues as to how the book should be interpreted. Ask questions such as:

1. What is the literary genre (e.g., law, poetry, narrative, history)?

2. How does it fit with the rest of the book? What does it add to the flow of the book?

3. What is its purpose and what does the author highlight?

4. Are there figures of speech that add to the complexity of the passage? Does Hebrew poetry aid in determining the meaning or purpose of the passage?

5. Is it a discussion, debate, conversation, or court scene? Is God speaking or the prophet and to whom?

6. Is the passage quoted or alluded to in other passages? (Use cross-reference Bibles and the "Index

of Quotations" and "Index of Allusions and Verbal Parallels" at the back of the most recent *The Greek New Testament* by the United Bible Societies. Another useful tool is Gleason L. Archer and Gregory C. Chirichigno, *Old Testament Quotations in the New Testament: A Complete Survey* [Chicago: Moody, 1983]).

Taking into account the type of literary genre can guide the overall interpretation. For instance, wisdom literature prompts the reader to think about a particular problem in a creative way and lets the reader draw his or her own conclusions. The book of Job is an excellent example. The question Job faces is how the retribution principle (i.e., that God blesses righteous people and punishes the wicked) can be correct when he is suffering. What Job does not know, but the reader does, is that he is facing a test—not a judgment. In this creative way the author leads the reader to question whether the retribution principle is sufficient to answer life's enigmas.

Redaction criticism examines how a text is ultimately put together by its final editors and how this structure relates to its meaning. Sometimes examining the structure can help delineate what units to preach. For example, Isaiah 5-12 follows a literary structure called a palistrophe (i.e., a literary structure in which the features in the first half of a passage correspond to features in the second half; similar to a chiasmus, but generally much larger).

A Song of judgment (Isa. 5:1-7)
   B Six "woes" pronounced upon the wicked (5:8-24)
      C An "uplifted hand" oracle culminating with the destruction by Assyria (5:25-30)
         D The Isaianic memoir (6:1-9:6[7])
      C' Four "uplifted hand" oracles culminating with the destruction by Assyria (9:7[8]-10:4)
   B' A "woe" pronounced upon Assyria (10:5-34) which gives rise to the restoration of Judah (11:1-16)
A' Song of thanksgiving (12:1-6)

This type of literary structure often highlights the middle unit, which is true here: the Isaianic memoir describes how God will bring about great deliverance for Israel. In this case, one (or more) sermon(s) could be dedicated to each of the sections of this literary structure. Not all Old Testament passages have an elaborate literary structure; nevertheless the structure should help determine the parameters of each section (or pericope).

Helpful Resources

LITERARY STRUCTURE

Bullinger, E. W. *Figures of Speech Used in the Bible: Explained and Illustrated.* London: Eyre & Spottiswoode, 1898. Reprint, Grand Rapids: Baker, 1977.

Ryken, Leland, et al., eds. *Dictionary of Biblical Imagery.* Downers Grove, IL: InterVarsity Press, 1998.

COMMENTARIES (IN THE INTRODUCTION ON LITERARY STRUCTURE)

Dorsey, David A. *The Literary Structure of the Old Testament: A Commentary on Genesis–Malachi.* Grand Rapids: Baker, 1999.

Eissfeldt, Otto. *The Old Testament: An Introduction.* New York: Harper and Row, 1965. See pages 9–127.

Sandy, D. Brent, and Ronald L. Giese, eds. *Cracking Old Testament Codes: A Guide to Interpreting Literary Genres of the Old Testament.* Nashville: Broadman and Holman, 1995.

Tucker, Gene M. *Form Criticism of the Old Testament.* Guides to Biblical Scholarship. Philadelphia: Fortress, 1971.

OLD TESTAMENT QUOTES IN THE NEW TESTAMENT

Archer, Gleason L., and Gregory C. Chirichigno, *Old Testament Quotations in the New Testament: A Complete Survey.* Chicago: Moody, 1983.

Beale, Gregory K., ed. *The Right Doctrine From the Wrong Texts? Essays on the Use of the Old Testament in the New.* Grand Rapids: Baker, 1994.

Bruce, F. F. *The New Testament Development of Old Testament Themes.* Grand Rapids: Eerdmans, 1969.

GENERAL DICTIONARIES/ENCYCLOPEDIAS/HANDBOOKS

Bromiley, Geoffrey W., ed. *The International Standard Bible Encyclopedia.* Revised edition. 4 vols. Grand Rapids: Eerdmans, 1979.

Douglas, James D., and N. Hillyer, eds. *The Illustrated Bible Dictionary.* 3 vols. Wheaton, IL: Tyndale House, 1980.

Freedman, David N. ed. *Anchor Bible Dictionary*. 6 vols.
New York: Doubleday, 1992.

6. *Highlight the Meanings of Words (Word Studies)*
Certain Hebrew words in a passage will be critical to
its understanding. Identify and examine key words carefully. A description of how to conduct a Hebrew word
study appears in appendix C, but this will not be necessary for most words. An important element of a word
study is to determine exactly what the word means in
context. This requires knowing the word's full range of
meaning. Hebrew concordances provide every occurrence
of specific Hebrew words in the Old Testament. Analyze
the context of each word. Then compare how it is used
in your passage. Also check the words used with it to determine its meaning more specifically. Then compare the
findings of this inductive study with Hebrew word study
books, theological dictionaries, or exegetical commentaries. Sometimes knowing the development of a word,
its semantic background, or its common usage may help
explain the meaning of the passage, as will as comparing
similar words. For example, the word *'almâ* used in Isaiah
7:14 emphasizes "youngness," while the word *betûlâ* emphasizes the idea of "virginity" (cf. Isa. 62:5).[3] Thus a reasonable translation of Isaiah 7:14b is "the young woman will
become pregnant and bear a son." Understanding how the
Hebrew word עַלְמָה *'almâ* "young woman" compares to בְּתוּלָה
betûlâ "virgin" helps us understand the author's choice of
this word in Isaiah 7:14.

Helpful Resources
LEXICONS/CONCORDANCES
Brown, Francis, S. R. Driver, and C. A. Briggs. *Hebrew and
English Lexicon of the Old Testament*. Oxford: Clarendon,
1906. Corrected by G. R. Driver, Oxford: Clarendon, 1951.
Reprint, Peabody, MA: Hendrickson, 1998.

---

3. The words *'almâ* and *betûlâ* have significant overlap in meaning, but
each word also has a specific nuance. Isaiah used *betûlâ* in 23:12, 37:22,
47:1, and 62:5 to refer to a "virgin"; thus one must ask why he used *'almâ*
in 7:14. The best answer is that Isaiah 7:14 uses *'almâ* to emphasize that
a "young woman" will be giving birth to a son during the time of Isaiah.
However, this verse is quoted in Matthew 1:22–23, where it is "filled up"
(*plēroō*) with meaning because it refers to Jesus.

Koehler, L., W. Baumgartner, and J. J. Stamm. *The Hebrew and Aramaic Lexicon of the Old Testament* [*HALOT*]. Translated and edited under the supervision of M. E. J. Richardson. 5 vols. Leiden: Brill, 1994–2000.

COMMENTARIES (FOR SPECIFIC WORD STUDY INFORMATION)
Even-Shoshan, Abraham. *A New Concordance of the Old Testament.* 2nd ed. Grand Rapids: Baker, 1989.
Wigram, George V. *The Englishman's Hebrew Concordance of the Old Testament.* Peabody, MA: Hendrickson, 1996.

WORD BOOKS/HEBREW DICTIONARIES
Harris, R. Laird, Gleason L. Archer Jr., and Bruce K. Waltke. *Theological Wordbook of the Old Testament.* Chicago: Moody, 2003.
Hatch, Edwin, and Henry A. Redpath. *Concordance to the Septuagint and Other Greek Versions of the Old Testament.* 3 vols. Oxford: Clarendon, 1897–1906. Reprint, Grand Rapids: Baker, 1998.
VanGemeren, Willem A., ed. *New International Dictionary of Old Testament Theology and Exegesis.* 5 vols. Grand Rapids: Zondervan, 1997.

BASIC OVERVIEW
Silva, Moisés. *Biblical Words and Their Meaning: An Introduction to Lexical Semantics. Revised edition.* Grand Rapids: Zondervan, 1995.
Vanhoozer, Kevin J. *Is There Meaning in This Text? The Bible, the Reader, and the Morality of Literary Knowledge.* Grand Rapids: Zondervan, 1998.

7. Examine the Syntax and Grammar
Because grammar critically affects interpretation, you should have a good grasp of the grammar and syntax of the passage you are studying. Carefully examine nuances of meaning in verb conjugations, prepositions, particles, and clause relationships. The summary of Hebrew grammar by Ronald Williams is extremely helpful here, especially the index of Hebrew words at the back. The biblical reference indexes in *Gesenius' Hebrew Grammar* and Waltke and O'Connor's *Introduction to Hebrew Syntax* can also help identify specific points of Hebrew grammar in your passage. Are there figures of speech or grammatical features

such as chiasm (i.e., an inverted sequence of phrases often signified by an a, b, b', a' pattern), ellipsis (i.e., an omission of words or a phrase; in English often signified by ". . ."), asyndeton (i.e., a stylistic construction in which conjunctions are omitted from a series of related clauses), protasis (i.e., the initial part of a conditional phrase; often begins with "if" in English), or anacoluthon (i.e., a rhetorical device signified by a change of syntax within a sentence or an abrupt change from one structure to another)? It is at this point that developing a syntactical outline as described in appendices D and E will be helpful. What is the main clause of the passage and how do other clauses relate to it? Draw arrows to indicate clause relationships and label the types of clauses (e.g., temporal, relative, causal). I cannot overemphasize the importance of a syntactical analysis. It provides the foundation for understanding a passage and developing your sermon. Difficult passages may have more than one way to outline the syntax, but at least you will be aware of the options and feasible interpretations. This will also help you rule out incorrect interpretations. Here again consulting reliable exegetical commentaries will allow you to compare your findings with those of other scholars.

An interesting grammatical nuance of a Hebrew verb can be found in Deuteronomy 24:4 where a rare Hothpael form is used to describe why a woman who has been divorced a second time cannot go back to her first husband. Apparently her first husband had her publicly disgraced and caused her "to regard herself as unclean."[4] Such an indignity would be very difficult to overlook or forgive. We are not told what the indecency was that caused the first husband to divorce her, but it was not so repulsive that another man would be unwilling to marry her. This understanding of the Hothpael verb stem aligns well with what Williams calls its "reflexive-estimative" usage.[5]

Helpful Resources
COMMENTARIES (GRAMMATICAL AND SYNTACTICAL INFORMATION)
Kautzsch, E. *Gesenius' Hebrew Grammar.* Translated by

---

4. See John H. Walton, "The Place of the Hutqattel Within the D-stem Group and Its Implications in Deuteronomy 24:4," *Hebrew Studies* 32 (1991): 7–17.
5. Ronald J. Williams, *Williams' Hebrew Syntax,* Revised and expanded by John C. Beckman, 3rd ed. (Toronto; Buffalo; London: University of Toronto Press, 2007), 64, par. 155.

A. E. Cowley. 2nd ed. Oxford: Oxford University Press, 1910. Especially the biblical passage index.
Waltke, Bruce K., and M. O'Connor. *An Introduction to Biblical Hebrew Syntax*. Winona Lake, IN: Eisenbrauns, 1990. Especially the biblical passage index.
Williams, Ronald J. *Williams' Hebrew Syntax*. Revised and expanded by John C. Beckman. 3rd ed. Toronto: University of Toronto Press, 2007. Especially the Hebrew words index on the last couple of pages of the book.

8. Begin Building the Sermon
Use your syntactical outline to develop the core of your sermon. The theme sentence from each paragraph (or strophe in poetry) should become the main points for your sermon. Each main point should be very applicable and meaningful to the people in your congregation. Your sermon preparation should include the following elements:
1. *The Title*. Develop a title that concisely captures the theme of the sermon. If the title is put on a church sign, think of a way to catch the interest of passersby. Think of what people are continually facing as challenges in their lives and how your passage might address them. Possible examples: "What You Should Know About Gossip," "Is Time Running Out?" "Where is God?" "If Life Is So Full, Why Do I Feel So Empty?" "Hurting at Home?" "Choose Your Friends Wisely," "Stress—When It's Good, and When It's Not," or "Money—Does Bill Gates Have Enough?"
2. *Introduction*. A good introduction captures the interest of your listeners and answers the question, "Why should I sit here for twenty to forty minutes (or more) and listen to what you have to say?" An anecdote that is relevant to the theme of your passage is often a good way to help listeners focus in on the topic. The introduction can make the difference between a memorable sermon and one that the listener tunes out after about ten minutes.
3. *Transitional Statement*. The transitional statement bridges the gap between the introduction of your sermon and the main points. It should contain a clear and specific key word, such as *reasons, consequences, lessons, principles,* or *guidelines*. This key word is important for creating a clear structure for the sermon. For example, "Psalm 23 contains three reasons why I can trust my Shepherd."

The main points are these three reasons—"I can trust my Shepherd because:

A. He is my Provider (vv. 1–3);
B. He is my Protector (vv. 4–5);
C. He is my Promise (v. 6)."

4. *Main Points.* The main points form the backbone of your sermon and provide the details of the biblical passage. In his classes Warren Wiersbe encourages soon-to-be-pastors to create main points that begin bridging the application gap between the biblical passage and the modern congregation. Take out historical references and include exhortations or principles that are memorable and applicable to your congregation.

5. *Conclusion.* The conclusion should review the main points of your passage and show how they point to one clear idea. If you cannot summarize the sermon in a single sentence, then rethink what you are trying to accomplish. This is your last opportunity to drive home this key point and make sure listeners understand what Scripture is telling them to do.

The transitional statement, key word, main points, and conclusion provide the structure of the sermon. For an example of this sermon structure see appendix E: "Syntactical Analysis of Psalm 23."

Helpful Resources
Blackwood, Andrew W. *The Preparation of Sermons.* New York; Nashville: Abingdon-Cokesbury, 1948. See pages 125–51.
Briscoe, D. Stuart. *Fresh Air in the Pulpit: Challenges and Encouragement from a Seasoned Preacher.* Grand Rapids: Baker, 1994.
Craddock, Fred B. *Preaching.* Nashville: Abingdon, 1985.
Demaray, Donald E., and George G. Hunter III. *Introduction to Homiletics.* 3rd ed. Indianapolis: Light and Life, 2006.
Koller, Charles W. *How to Preach Without Notes.* Grand Rapids: Baker, 2007.
MacArthur, John, et al. *Rediscovering Expository Preaching: Balancing the Science and Art of Biblical Exposition.* Dallas: Word, 1992.

Perry, Lloyd M. *Biblical Sermon Guide: How to Prepare and Present a Biblical Sermon.* Grand Rapids: Baker, 1970.

Robinson, Haddon W. *Biblical Preaching: The Development and Delivery of Expository Messages.* 2nd ed. Grand Rapids: Baker, 2001.

Sunukjian, Donald R. *Invitation to Biblical Preaching: Proclaiming Truth with Clarity and Relevance.* Grand Rapids: Kregel, 2007.

9. Observe Theological Issues

Sermons should help listeners build a personal theology, the biblical grid that helps us make everyday decisions about how to live our lives in ways that please God. Every sermon should add something to this personal theology and contribute to a strong foundation for all of life's decisions. For example, the Bible speaks a lot about marriage; in fact, the idea of two people becoming one was God's. So what can I learn about marriage from the Bible? What is its purpose? What does the Bible say about how I should treat my spouse? What is my job as a husband or wife? What about divorce?

Over the years exegetical sermons will hopefully provide the answers to these relevant questions and gradually help people build their personal theology. However, we need to be intentional in helping to build a personal theology by clearly explaining how biblical principles apply to specific situations. We need to address questions such as: How does this passage apply to us today? How do these biblical principles affect my core beliefs? How does the message of a biblical book or passage fit into the rest of my personal theology?

A good example of this principle can be found in Habakkuk chapter 1 where God informs Habakkuk that He will allow the ruthless Babylonians to punish the Israelites. Habakkuk's immediate response is, How can a righteous, loving God stand back and watch as the wicked Babylonians destroy those who are more righteous than they? We see that Habakkuk's core beliefs about God and how He acts have been severely shaken. God's response to Habakkuk applies to both the Babylonians, as well as himself. In Habakkuk 2:4 God says, "Behold, as for the proud one, his soul is not right within him; but the righteous will live by his faith."

On the one hand, following the flow of thought in the book, the "proud one" signifies the Babylonians. God had already proclaimed, "They will be held guilty, they whose strength is their god" (Hab. 1:11). On the other hand, Habakkuk can also be considered a "proud one." He had just been telling God how poorly He was running the world—He does not listen to His children (1:2); He lets wickedness go unpunished so justice is perverted (1:4); and He is silent while the wicked "swallow up" those more righteous than they (1:13). In effect, Habakkuk thinks he can do a better job of running the world than God—a prideful attitude indeed. Habakkuk has to learn to sit back and trust that this amazing God knows what He is doing. We too, experience times when we think we can run our lives and our world better than God. God's message to the Babylonians, Habakkuk, and to us is that "the righteous one will live by his [or her] faith." Do we trust God to bring about justice in our lives and on the earth? Do we trust Him to know what He is doing when things look out of control? It takes faith to place our trust in God and then let Him do what is best. What an amazing principle this adds to our personal theology: God knows what He is doing even though I only see a small part of the big picture.

Helpful Resources
COMMENTARIES (INTRODUCTIONS USUALLY INCLUDE A SECTION ON THE THEOLOGY OF THE BOOK)
Elwell, Walter A., ed. *Evangelical Dictionary of Biblical Theology*. Grand Rapids: Baker, 1996.
Erickson, Millard J. *Christian Theology*. 2nd ed. Grand Rapids: Baker, 1998.
Grudem, Wayne. *Systematic Theology*. Grand Rapids: Zondervan, 1994.
House, Paul R. *Old Testament Theology*. Downers Grove, IL: InterVarsity Press, 1998.
Kaiser, Walter C. *Toward an Old Testament Theology*. Grand Rapids: Zondervan, 1978.
———. *Toward Old Testament Ethics*. Grand Rapids: Zondervan, 1983.

10. Offer Clear Illustrations and Application
Howard Hendricks tells of a survey of 4,000 laymen in 114 evangelical churches across the U.S. who were asked,

"Do you feel the preaching on Sunday relates to what's going on in your life?" Over 83 percent saw virtually no connection between what they heard on Sunday morning and what they faced on Monday morning.[6] This statistic is from more than twenty years ago, but I doubt that it is significantly better today. Helping your listeners bridge the gap between Sunday morning and Monday morning is critical. Nineteenth century pastor Robert W. Dale, in his Yale lectures on preaching, underscores this importance:

> An English preacher of the last generation used to say that he cared very little what he said the first half hour, but he cared a very great deal what he said the last fifteen minutes. I remember reading many years ago an address published to students by Henry Ward Beecher, in which he gave a very striking account of a sermon by Jonathan Edwards. Beecher says that in the elaborated doctrinal part of Jonathan Edwards' sermon the great preacher was only getting his guns into position, but that in his applications he opened fire on the enemy. There are too many of us, I am afraid, who take so much time getting our guns into position that we have to finish without firing a shot. We say that we leave the truth to do its own work. We trust to the hearts and consciences of our hearers to apply it. Depend upon it, gentlemen, this is a great and fatal mistake.[7]

Carefully examine the passage to identify timeless principles. Decide what type of response you expect from someone in the congregation and focus on that application. The application must be clear, specific, and positive. If it is negative—that is, something that must not be done—then clearly explain how to avoid doing it and what should be done instead.

The application process helps take people from passive listening, from thinking "that's interesting," to actively engaging the realization that "I need that for my life."

---

6. Howard Hendricks, 1984 Multnomah Pastor's Enrichment Conference.
7. G. Campbell Morgan, *Preaching* (Grand Rapids: Baker, 1979), 87–88.

Sir Francis Bacon says it this way:

> It is not what men eat but what they digest that makes them strong; not what we gain but what we save that makes us rich; not what we read but what we remember that makes us learned; not what we preach but what we practice that makes us Christians.[8]

Helpful Resources

Blackwood, Andrew W. *The Preparation of Sermons.* New York; Nashville: Abingdon-Cokesbury, 1948. See pages 152–61, 243–51.

Briscoe, D. Stuart. *Fresh Air in the Pulpit: Challenges and Encouragement from a Seasoned Preacher.* Grand Rapids: Baker, 1994. See pages 139–55.

Broadus, John A. *On the Preparation and Delivery of Sermons,* revised by Vernon L. Stanfield. 4th ed. San Francisco: Harper San Francisco, 1979. See pages 196–209.

Demaray, Donald E., and George G. Hunter III. *Introduction to Homiletics.* 3rd ed. Indianapolis: Light and Life, 2006. See pages 139–54.

Lloyd-Jones, D. Martyn. *Preaching and Preachers.* Grand Rapids: Zondervan, 1971. See pages 224–43.

MacArthur, John, et al. *Rediscovering Expository Preaching: Balancing the Science and Art of Biblical Exposition.* Dallas: Word, 1992. See pages 242–54.

Robinson, Haddon W. *Biblical Preaching: The Development and Delivery of Expository Messages.* 2nd ed. Grand Rapids: Baker, 2001. See pages 137–56.

Spurgeon, Charles H. *Lectures to My Students.* Grand Rapids: Zondervan, 1979. See pages 349–443.

Wiersbe, Warren W., and Lloyd M. Perry. *The Wycliffe Handbook of Preaching and Preachers.* Chicago: Moody, 1984. See pages 179–82.

11. Keep Prayer a Priority

Remember to pray carefully over all parts of the sermon, for unless God adds the power, the application will fall flat. Charles H. Spurgeon knew how vital prayer is (see next page).

---

8. Francis Bacon, "Application," in Sermon Illustrations, http://www.sermonillustrations.com/a-z/a/application.htm (accessed October 1, 2006).

Five young college students were spending a Sunday in London, so they went to hear the famed C. H. Spurgeon preach. While waiting for the doors to open, the students were greeted by a man who asked, "Gentlemen, let me show you around. Would you like to see the heating plant of this church?" They were not particularly interested, for it was a hot day in July. But they didn't want to offend the stranger, so they consented. The young men were taken down a stairway, a door was quietly opened, and their guide whispered, "This is our heating plant." Surprised, the students saw 700 people bowed in prayer, seeking a blessing on the service that was soon to begin in the auditorium above. Softly closing the door, the gentleman then introduced himself. It was none other than Charles Spurgeon.[9]

Many Christians have lost sight of the importance of prayer. Without God's power, the sermon will remain lifeless, no matter how accurate and polished it is. Equally, simply listening to a sermon is not what brings lasting change. We need to ask God's Spirit to use His truth to change lives.

Helpful Resources

Craddock, Fred B. *Preaching*. Nashville: Abingdon, 1985. See pages 51–65.

Demaray, Donald E., and George G. Hunter III. *Introduction to Homiletics*. 3rd ed. Indianapolis: Light and Life, 2006. See pages 182–88.

Lloyd-Jones, D. Martyn. *Preaching and Preachers*. Grand Rapids: Zondervan, 1971. See pages 169–71.

MacArthur, John, et al. *Rediscovering Expository Preaching:*

---

9. *Our Daily Bread* April 24. Quoted from "Sermon Illustrations," http://www.sermonillustrations.com/a-z/p/prayer.htm (accessed October 1, 2006).

Balancing the Science and Art of Biblical Exposition.
Dallas: Word, 1992. See pages 63–84.
Müller, George. *A Narrative of Some of the Lord's Dealings
with George Müller.* 2 vols. Muskegon, MI: Dust & Ashes,
2003. See 1:50–51, 2:740–41, 762, 773.
Spurgeon, Charles H. *Lectures to My Students.* Grand
Rapids: Zondervan, 1979. See pages 42–69.

CONCLUSION

Just as a house cannot be built without a detailed plan, so
it is with a sermon. The structure laid out above can provide
the detailed plan for building an exegetical sermon. The steps
can be rearranged and modified to make them your own, but
each is important in providing part of the foundation necessary to expound the Word of God completely and with power.
The acrostic "READ THE BOOK" is one way to help you remember and implement the various parts of the exegetical
process.

THINGS TO CONSIDER

1. Do you see what each step of sermon preparation
   contributes to the final product? Are there any you
   need to give more attention to?

2. Are you willing to commit the time to consistently
   prepare God's Word for your congregation?

3. Do you understand the importance of expository
   preaching?

FURTHER READING

Blackwood, Andrew W. *The Preparation of Sermons.* New
York; Nashville: Abingdon-Cokesbury, 1948.
Gibson, Scott M., ed. *Preaching the Old Testament.* Grand
Rapids: Baker, 2006.
Koller, Charles W. *How to Preach Without Notes.* Grand
Rapids: Baker, 2007.
Parker, Don. *Using Biblical Hebrew in Ministry: A Practical
Guide for Pastors, Seminarians, and Bible Students.*
Lanham, MD: University Press of America, 1995.
Robinson, Haddon W. *Biblical Preaching: The Development
and Delivery of Expository Messages.* 2nd ed. Grand
Rapids: Baker, 2001.

Stuart, Douglas. *Old Testament Exegesis: A Handbook for Students and Pastors.* 3rd ed. Louisville: Westminster John Knox, 2001.

Sunukjian, Donald R. *Invitation to Biblical Preaching: Proclaiming Truth with Clarity and Relevance.* Grand Rapids: Kregel, 2007.

CHAPTER
FIVE

MAKING EXEGESIS
PRACTICAL

HOW DO I REAP THE BENEFITS
OF ALL THE LABOR OF LEARNING HEBREW?

Bible study is like jogging. Getting started
is always the hardest part.

—Paul D. Wegner

D an pulls into the church parking lot about 9:00 o'clock every weekday morning and, just like the pastor of every other smaller church, he is very busy. However, he made a commitment when he was in seminary to translate the biblical texts from the original Hebrew or Greek texts before preaching them. Dan admits that this has not always been easy and at times he has had to make compromises, but generally speaking he has stuck to his commitment. He also admits that his translating has gotten significantly faster and his preaching much deeper. Even his congregation has noticed the improvement and some people drive for quite a distance to hear good, biblical exposition. Dan is a living example that it is possible to keep up with your biblical languages in the pastorate, but it starts with a commitment. His advice to seminary students is: "Keep up your Hebrew and do not let it gradually slip away from you," and to pastors who have already allowed it to slip away: "Set aside a time to begin to work through a Hebrew grammar and if at all possible take a Hebrew refresher class at a seminary." Dan believes it is crucial to his ministry to continue study in the original languages so he can feed his sheep the best exegetical sermons possible—that has been his goal for about seven years now.

This chapter offers a variety of suggestions to maintain and even advance your Hebrew skills. It is divided into three sections: (1) maintaining Hebrew translation skills, (2) retaining Hebrew vocabulary, and (3) how to keep using Hebrew in your sermons.

MAINTAINING HEBREW TRANSLATION SKILLS

I believe that one of the primary reasons that we do not keep up our Hebrew is that we have not determined to make it a priority. This may be because we do not recognize its value, other priorities have crowded it out, or we do not know Hebrew well enough to keep it up. But whatever it is, we need to make a firm commitment to keep using our Hebrew. My Hebrew teacher, Dennis R. Magary, states it a slightly different way:

> Learning biblical Hebrew is a challenge. But learning the language is not the greatest challenge. Academic incentive is a great motivator. As long as there are quizzes to take and exercises to write, as long as there is a grade riding on what you do, and there is a professor to whom you must give account, staying with the language and succeeding somehow stays within reach. But what happens when there are no longer quizzes or exercises or professors or grades?[1]

When you initially started Hebrew, it was probably because someone else made the decision for you. Either your school required biblical languages for a specific program or someone told you it was necessary. But at some point it will become your decision to keep using the language. Here are some suggestions to help you do just that.

There are approximately 23,145 verses in the Old Testament. If you translate three verses a day, it would take

---

1. Dennis R. Magary, "Keeping Your Hebrew Healthy," in *Preaching the Old Testament*, ed. Scott M. Gibson (Grand Rapids: Baker, 2006), 29.

you a little over twenty-one years (7,715 days) to complete the Old Testament—obviously, six verses would take about ten-and-a-half years and nine verses would be about seven years. This is certainly overwhelming, but certain passages are much more important than others to translate and I suggest you center on those. The list of Old Testament books on the following page indicates about how long it would take to translate each book at three verses a day:

Idea: It can be overwhelming to think of translating the entire Old Testament. Shift your focus by picking some of the smaller books to get started. My recommendations would be Ruth (about a month), Esther (about a month and a half), Habakkuk (almost 3 weeks), Haggai (about 2 weeks), or Malachi (almost 3 weeks). These books are manageable in size and have good potential for very interesting sermons.

Idea: Choose a single longer book like Genesis and determine to spend about a year and a half translating and preaching it. Start the translation process early so that you can be well ahead of your sermon preparation. Psalms is the only book that is longer than Genesis.

Idea: Why not get together several seminary friends and work on translating various books? This would encourage all of you to keep going. Make sure that you all have the same format and structure; then share your translations. Either you could all translate different parts of a large book, or each choose a different shorter book. When each has completed their work, get together and check it. If three people work on the book of Genesis at three verses a day, you could complete a translation in only 57 days.

Idea: Share your desire to keep up your Hebrew with another Hebrew student (or former student). You may not choose to translate three verses a day, but you can at least hold each other accountable to do some translating in the Hebrew text. Preach

BIBLICAL BOOK	VERSES	TIME (DAYS AT THREE VERSES A DAY)	BIBLICAL BOOK	VERSES	TIME (DAYS AT THREE VERSES A DAY)
Genesis	1,533	511	Ecclesiastes	222	74
Exodus	1,213	405	Song of Solomon	117	39
Leviticus	859	287	Isaiah	1,292	431
Numbers	1,288	430	Jeremiah	1,364	455
Deuteronomy	959	320	Lamentations	154	52
Joshua	658	220	Ezekiel	1,273	425
Judges	618	206	Daniel	357	119
Ruth	85	29	Hosea	197	66
1 Samuel	810	270	Joel	73	25
2 Samuel	695	232	Amos	146	49
1 Kings	816	272	Obadiah	21	7
2 Kings	719	240	Jonah	48	16
1 Chronicles	942	314	Micah	105	35
2 Chronicles	822	274	Nahum	47	16
Ezra	280	94	Habakkuk	56	19
Nehemiah	406	136	Zephaniah	53	18
Esther	167	56	Haggai	38	13
Job	1,070	357	Zechariah	211	71
Psalms	2,461	821	Malachi	55	19
Proverbs	915	305	Total:	23,145	7,715

through an Old Testament book and share your findings with your friend as you go. Mutually sharing what you glean from your work will be an encouragement to you both.

Idea: Check one of the literal translations of the Bible against the Hebrew text and make marginal notes instead of writing a new translation. Wide-margined Bibles are useful so you can make notes beside each verse. This should take about half as long as making a completely new translation. In the end you will have a Bible that you have personally checked for accuracy which can be used for preaching and teaching.

Idea: If you don't have time to check a translation, at least read the definitions of the major Hebrew words in a Hebrew lexicon. Write notes about key elements of these words in the margins of your Bible. Because Hebrew is a very picturesque language, you can gain a great deal of insight into the meaning of the text by merely examining the meanings of the nouns. One of my former students loved to study Hebrew vocabulary and read much of the BDB lexicon. I was amazed how much information he picked up about the Hebrew text based primarily on the meanings of the Hebrew nouns. You can also examine verbs and nuances of meaning of their various stems, but the nouns will probably provide more useful information.

Idea: Could it be possible that someone in your congregation would like to learn Hebrew? Teaching it is the best way to maintain it and continue learning right along with them. Even teaching the basics of Hebrew grammar and how to use some Hebrew study tools can help someone dig more deeply in their Bible study.

RETAINING HEBREW VOCABULARY

Eugene H. Merrill states: "I believe learning vocabulary is probably the biggest hindrance for people retaining their Hebrew, since it gets very discouraging to have to look up so many unknown words."[2] There are about 8,390 Hebrew words and 1,100 Aramaic words in the Old Testament. However, only about 680 Hebrew words are used 50 times or more, and these are the ones you should focus on. By knowing the words occurring 50 times or more, you can pick up your Hebrew Old Testament and only have to look up about 20 percent of the words. This also means that about 7,700 Hebrew words occur fewer than 50 times, so for most people it is probably not worth the effort to memorize these. Biblical Hebrew actually has far fewer words than English. The English language contains about one million words of which an average educated person knows about 20,000[3] and uses only about 2,000 different words a week.[4] That is far more than the common Hebrew words. Nevertheless, Hebrew vocabulary can be particularly difficult for most people to remember. Here are some suggestions:

Idea: Some people find that studying Hebrew vocabulary right before going to bed allows your brain to continue processing what they studied. To assist your memory, you can group together Hebrew words that are related (i.e., verbs [אָכַל "to eat"] and nouns [אֹכֶל "food"]) or that look similar but are different (i.e., אַחַר "after" and אַחֵר "another").

Idea: Study vocabulary with a friend. Each person seems to remember different Hebrew vocabulary, so quiz each other to retain words you know well and better learn those you don't.

Idea: A simple vocabulary program for computers and iPods is available so students can study Hebrew vocabulary whenever they have a few spare minutes.[5] Other help for vocabulary currently available is "Basics of Biblical Hebrew Vocabulary Audio" by

2. Personal conversation at National ETS conference 2006.
3. Glenn Elert, ed., "Number of Words in the English Language," http://hypertextbook.com/facts/2001/JohnnyLing.shtml (accessed August 8, 2007).
4. Ibid.
5. David M. Hoffeditz and J. Michael Thigpen, *iVocab Biblical Hebrew 2.0: See and Hear Flashcards for Your MP3 Player, Cell Phone, and Computer* (DVD-ROM) (Grand Rapids: Kregel, 2008).

Gary D. Pratico and Jonathan T. Pennington (available through Zondervan).

Idea: Develop your own vocabulary "games" to play with a friend. For instance, my students have played my version of "Parseword," patterned after the classic game Password. Played in pairs, one student has a card with a Hebrew verb to parse and the other student holds a card with the correct answer. The student with the Hebrew verb tries to figure out its parsing and their partner answers "yes" or "no" until they get it right. This can also be done with vocabulary words and definitions.

Idea: Put up creative posters around your church with important Hebrew words and their meanings. If done well, it will not only reinforce the meanings of the words, but will create interest in the congregation to learn more about Hebrew.

Idea: Learn Hebrew words in order of their usage so that you are very familiar with the 97 words that occur more than 500 times. Next learn the 121 words that occur between 200 to 500 times, and so on. Learning Hebrew words in order of occurrence will ensure that you know the most common Hebrew words. The most common Hebrew words can be found in: Miles V. Van Pelt and Gary D. Pratico, *The Vocabulary Guide to Biblical Hebrew* (Grand Rapids: Zondervan, 2003); George M. Landes, *Building Your Biblical Hebrew Vocabulary* (Atlanta: Society of Biblical Literature, 2001); or Larry A. Mitchell, *A Student's Vocabulary for Biblical Hebrew and Aramaic* (Grand Rapids: Zondervan, 1984).

Idea: Try to learn Hebrew vocabulary the way a child learns English. Find the Hebrew words for fifty objects around your home or school and learn them by associating the name with the object (vocabulary cards can be placed on or near these objects). Next find the Hebrew verbs for twenty common actions and learn them.

HOW TO KEEP USING HEBREW IN YOUR SERMONS

Scott M. Gibson gives a variety of reasons why pastors rarely preach from the Old Testament. These reasons range from "Hebrew is harder than Greek" to "It is such a foreign culture that it is difficult to apply it to modern congregations."[6] There may be some truth in each of these reasons, but it's worth the extra time to delve into the Old Testament since it provides a foundation for much of what is taught in the New Testament.

I am convinced that the best way to make sure you'll keep using your Hebrew is to preach various series from the Old Testament. Start with shorter books and prepare as suggested above. Even small steps like checking a literal translation of the Bible against the Hebrew text before you preach it or doing a couple of word studies, would improve your understanding of the passage.

Idea: Choose three Old Testament books that you could preach. Shorter books (e.g., Jonah, Ruth, and Esther) are a good beginning and will provide a foundation to build upon.

Idea: If preaching through a whole book seems too daunting, then choose several psalms or proverbs for a preaching series. Even if you choose very short psalms and translate them from the Hebrew text, you will begin to deepen your sermons.

Idea: Teach a Sunday school class or adult enrichment class on an Old Testament book. Make sure to translate the most important parts of the book and examine the historical background, literary structure, and grammatical features. This will provide much of the background for a sermon series that you could prepare next. By planning ahead you may be able to overlap much of your preparation and save yourself valuable time.

Idea: Use every tool at your disposal to help translate

---

6. Scott M. Gibson, "Challenges to Preaching the Old Testament," in *Preaching the Old Testament*, ed. Scott M. Gibson (Grand Rapids: Baker, 2006), 21–26.

and understand Old Testament passages before you preach. This is where computer programs, Hebrew lexicons, and Hebrew concordances come in.

Idea: Take a refresher class in Hebrew or read through a Hebrew grammar. If there is anyone locally who is proficient in Hebrew (possibly at a seminary or synagogue), either take a class with him or her or at least arrange to ask them questions on an as-needed basis. Personal one-on-one contact is best when learning Hebrew, but there are also good books and CDs (e.g., Parson's "Hebrew Tutor Interactive Learning System"; Russell Fuller's *Invitation to Biblical Hebrew* comes with a DVD video series) to help you learn Hebrew better. Sometimes it just takes hearing something a second time or in a different way to actually "get it."

Idea: Overlap your sermon preparation with your daily devotions. Translate the biblical text and then think of the ways it can be properly applied. Translating from the Hebrew text (or Greek text for that matter) will add depth and accuracy to your understanding of the passage.

CONCLUSION

Some seminaries and Bible schools have required their students to take at least a year or two of Hebrew because they consider it a prerequisite for becoming a good pastor, and I agree. But now the decision is up to you. You can let all the time and effort that you have invested in Hebrew go the same way as your high school Spanish or French classes, or you can use some of the ideas listed above to continue with your Hebrew and even help it grow. I pray that you will choose the latter so that pulpits will again be filled with knowledgeable preachers of the Old Testament.

THINGS TO CONSIDER

1. What would it take for you to start using your Hebrew for sermon preparation? Are the benefits worth the cost?

2. Which suggestions listed above could improve your chances of using Hebrew in your ministry? Is there anyone who could hold you accountable?

3. Is there anyone in your congregation who could take over one or two of your responsibilities in order to free up more time for delving into the Hebrew text?

FURTHER READING

Gibson, Scott M., ed. *Preaching the Old Testament*. Grand Rapids: Baker, 2006.

Kaiser, Walter C. *Preaching and Teaching from the Old Testament: A Guide for the Church*. Grand Rapids: Baker, 2003.

OLD TESTAMENT COMMENTARIES

A multipage table of Old Testament commentaries follows, divided into scholarly and lay categories and defined by theological persuasion.

BIBLICAL BOOK	SCHOLARLY COMMENTARIES		LAY COMMENTARIES
	NON-EVANGELICAL	EVANGELICAL	EVANGELICAL
Genesis	1. Westermann, C. *Genesis 1–11; 12–36; 37–50: A Commentary.* Augsburg, 1985. 2. Sarna, N. *Genesis.* JPSTC. JPS, 1989.	1. Wenham, G. J. *Genesis 1–15; Genesis 16–50.* WBC 1, 2. Word, 1987, 1994. 2. Waltke, B. K., and C. Fredricks. *Genesis: A Commentary.* Zondervan, 2001. 3. Hamilton, V. P. *Genesis 1–17; Genesis 18–50.* NICOT. Eerdmans, 1990, 1995.	1. Walton, J. H. *Genesis.* NIVAC. Zondervan, 2001. 2. Baldwin, J. *The Message of Genesis 12–50.* InterVarsity, 1986. 3. Sailhamer, John H. "Genesis," EBC, Zondervan, 1990 (2:3–284).
Exodus	1. Sarna, N. *Exodus.* JPSTC. JPS, 1991. 2. Childs, Brevard. *The Book of Exodus.* OTL. Westminster, 1974. 3. Propp, W. H. C. *Exodus 1–18.* AB 2. Doubleday, 1998.	1. Durham, J. I. *Exodus.* WBC 3. Word, 1987. 2. Cole, R. A. *Exodus.* TOTC 2. InterVarsity, 1973. 3. Cassuto, U. *A Commentary on the Book of Exodus.* Magnes, 1967.	1. Kaiser, W. C. "Exodus," EBC. Zondervan, 1990 (2:287–497). 2. Enns, Peter. *Exodus.* NIVAC. Zondervan, 2000.
Leviticus	1. Milgrom, J. *Leviticus 1–16; Leviticus 17–22; Leviticus 23–27.* AB 3–3B. Doubleday, 1991, 2000, 2001. 2. Levine, B. A. *Leviticus.* JPSTC. JPS, 1989.	1. Hartley, J. E. *Leviticus.* WBC 4. Word, 1992. 2. Wenham, G. J. *The Book of Leviticus.* NICOT. Eerdmans, 1979. 3. Rooker, Mark F. *Leviticus.* NAC. Broadman and Holman, 2000.	1. Harrison, R. K. *Leviticus.* TOTC. InterVarsity, 1980. 2. Harris, R. L. "Leviticus." EBC. Zondervan, 1990 (2:501–645). 3. Ross, A. P. *Holiness to the Lord: A Guide to the Exposition of the Book of Leviticus.* Baker, 2002.
Numbers	1. Levine, B. A. *Numbers 1–20, 21–36.* AB 4–4a. Doubleday, 1993, 2000. 2. Milgrom, J. *Numbers.* JPSTC. JPS, 1990.	1. Ashley, T. R. *Numbers.* NICOT. Eerdmans, 1993. 2. Cole, R. D. *Numbers.* NAC 3B. Broadman and Holman, 2000.	1. Allen, R. B. "Numbers," EBC. Zondervan, 1990 (2:657–1008). 2. Wenham, G. J. *Numbers.* TOTC 4. InterVarsity, 1981.

(continued)

BIBLICAL BOOK	SCHOLARLY COMMENTARIES		LAY COMMENTARIES
	NON-EVANGELICAL	EVANGELICAL	EVANGELICAL
Deuteronomy	1. Weinfeld, M. *Deuteronomy 1–11*. AB 5. Doubleday, 1991. 2. Tigay, J. *Deuteronomy*. JPSTC. JPS, 1996. 3. von Rad, G. *Deuteronomy*. OTL. Westminster, 1966.	1. Craigie, P. C. *The Book of Deuteronomy*. NICOT. Eerdmans, 1976. 2. Christiansen, D. L. *Deuteronomy 1–11*. WBC 6A. Eerdmans, 1991. 3. Merrill, E. H. *Deuteronomy*. NAC 4. Broadman and Holman, 1994.	1. Thompson, J. A. *Deuteronomy*. TOTC 5. InterVarsity, 1974. 2. Brown, R. *The Message of Deuteronomy*. InterVarsity, 1993.
Joshua	1. Boling, R. *Joshua*. AB 6. Doubleday, 1982. 2. Butler, T. C. *Joshua*. WBC 7. Word, 1993. 3. Nelson, R. D. *Joshua: A Commentary*. OTL. John Knox, 1997.	1. Woudstra, M. *The Book of Joshua*. NICOT. Eerdmans, 1981. 2. Howard, D. M. *Joshua*. NAC 5. Broadman and Holman, 1999.	1. Hess, R. *Joshua* TOTC 6. InterVarsity, 1996. 2. Waltke, B. "The Book of Joshua," NBC: 21st Century Edition. InterVarsity, 1994.
Judges	1. Boling, R. *Judges*. AB 6A. Doubleday, 1975. 2. Burney, C. F. *Judges and Kings*. 1903; Reprint KTAV, 1970. 3. Lindars, B. *Judges 1–5: A New Translation and Commentary*. T. & T. Clark, 1995.	1. Block, D. *Judges, Ruth*. NAC 6. Broadman, 1999. 2. Cundall, A., and L. Morris. *Judges and Ruth*. TOTC 7. InterVarsity, 1968.	1. Bruce, F. F. "Judges" NBC. Rev. ed. Eerdmans, 1970.
Ruth	1. Campbell, E. F. *Ruth*. AB 7. Doubleday, 1975. 2. Sasson, J. M. *Ruth*. Johns Hopkins, 1979.	1. Hubbard, R. L. *The Book of Ruth*. NICOT. Eerdmans, 1988. 2. Block, D. *Judges, Ruth*. NAC 6. Broadman and Holman, 1999. 3. Bush, F. W. *Ruth, Esther*. WBC 9. Word, 1996.	1. Cundall, A., and L. Morris. *Judges and Ruth*. TOTC 7. InterVarsity, 1968.

(continued)	SCHOLARLY COMMENTARIES		LAY COMMENTARIES
BIBLICAL BOOK	NON-EVANGELICAL	EVANGELICAL	EVANGELICAL
1-2 Samuel	1. McCarter, P. K. *2 Samuel*. AB 8, 9. Doubleday, 1980, 1984. 2. Hertzberg, H. W. *I & II Samuel: A Commentary*. OTL. Westminster, 1964.	1. Bergen, R. D. *1, 2 Samuel*. NAC 7. Broadman and Holman, 1996. 2. Klein, R. W. *1 Samuel*. WBC 10. Word, 1983. 3. Anderson, A. A. *2 Samuel*. WBC 11. Word, 1989.	1. Baldwin, J. G. *1 and 2 Samuel*. TOTC 8. InterVarsity, 1988. 2. Gordon, R. P. *I and II Samuel*. Zondervan, 1986.
1-2 Kings	1. Cogan, M., J. *First Kings*. AB 10. Doubleday, 2001. 2. Cogan, M., and H. Tadmor. *Second Kings*. AB 11. Doubleday, 1988. 3. Montgomery, J. A. *Critical and Exegetical Commentary on the Books of Kings*. ICC. T. & T. Clark, 1951.	1. DeVries, Simon J. *1 Kings*. WBC 12. Word, 1985. 1. Hobbs, T. R. *2 Kings*. WBC 13. Word, 1985. 3. Provan, I. W. *First and Second Kings*. NIBC 7. Hendrickson, 1995.	1. Wiseman, D. J. *1 & 2 Kings*. TOTC 9. InterVarsity, 1993. 2. House, P. R. *First and Second Kings*. NAC 8. Broadman and Holman, 1995.
1-2 Chronicles	1. Japhet, S. *I and II Chronicles*. OTL. Westminster/John Knox, 1993. 2. Myers, J. M. *First Chronicles; Second Chronicles*. AB 12, 13. Doubleday, 1986. 3. Williamson, H. G. M. *I and II Chronicles*. NCB. Eerdmans, 1982.	1. Braun, R. *1 Chronicles*. WBC 14. Word, 1986. 2. Dillard, R. B. *2 Chronicles*. WBC 15. Word, 1987. 3. Thompson, J. A. *1, 2 Chronicles*. NAC 9. Broadman and Holman, 1994.	1. Selman, M. *1 and 2 Chronicles*. TOTC 10a, 10b. InterVarsity, 1994. 2. McConville, J. G. *I & II Chronicles*. DSB. Westminster, 1984.
Ezra–Nehemiah	1. Myers, J. M. *Ezra–Nehemiah*. AB 14. Doubleday, 1965. 2. Blinkinsopp, J. *Ezra–Nehemiah: A Commentary*. OTL. Westminster, 1988. 3. Clines, David J. A. *Ezra, Nehemiah, Esther*. NCB. Eerdmans, 1984.	1. Fensham, F. C. *The Books of Ezra and Nehemiah*. NICOT. Eerdmans, 1982. 2. Williamson, H. G. M. *Ezra, Nehemiah*. WBC 16. Word, 1985.	1. Kidner, D. *Ezra & Nehemiah*. TOTC 11. InterVarsity, 1979. 2. Yamauchi, E. M. "Ezra and Nehemia." EBC. Zondervan, 1988 (4:546–771).

(continued)

BIBLICAL BOOK	SCHOLARLY COMMENTARIES		LAY COMMENTARIES
	NON-EVANGELICAL	EVANGELICAL	EVANGELICAL
Esther	1. Moore, C. *Esther.* AB 7B. Doubleday, 1971. 2. Clines, D. J. A. *Ezra, Nehemiah, Esther.* NCB. Eerdmans, 1984. 3. Levenson, Jon D. *Esther: A Commentary.* OTL. Westminster John Knox, 1997.	1. Bush, F. *Ruth and Esther.* WBC 9. Word, 1996. 2. Baldwin, J. G. *Esther.* TOTC 12. InterVarsity, 1984.	1. Jobes, Karen H. *Esther.* NIVAC. Zondervan, 1999. 2. Huey, F. B. "Esther." EBC. Zondervan, 1988 (4:775–839).
Job	1. Pope, M. *Job.* AB 15. Doubleday, 1965. 2. Gordis, R. *The Book of Job: Commentary, New Translation, and Special Studies.* JTS Press, 1978. 3. Habel, N. C. *The Book of Job: A Commentary.* OTL. Westminster, 1985.	1. Hartley, J. *The Book of Job.* NICOT. Eerdmans, 1988. 2. Clines, D. J. A. *Job 1–20; Job 21–40.* WBC 17, 18. Word, 1996.	1. Anderson, F. I. *Job.* TOTC 13. InterVarsity, 1976. 2. Atkinson, D. *The Message of Job.* InterVarsity, 1991.
Psalms	1. Kraus, Hans-J. *Psalms 1–59; 60–150.* Augsburg, 1988, 1989. 2. Anderson, A. A. *Psalms.* NCB. 2 Vols. Eerdmans, 1972. 3. Mays, J. L. *Psalms.* Interp. John Knox, 1994.	1. Craigie, P. *Psalms 1–50.* WBC 19. Word, 1983. 2. Tate, M. E. *Psalms 51–100.* WBC 20. Word, 1991. 3. Allen, L. *Psalms 101–150.* WBC 21. Word, 1983.	1. Kidner, D. *Psalms: An Introduction and Commentary.* 2 vols. TOTC 14. InterVarsity, 1973–75. 2. Lewis, C. S. *Reflections on the Psalms.* Harcourt, 1958. 3. Longman, T. *How to Read the Psalms.* InterVarsity, 1988.
Proverbs	1. Scott, R. B. Y. *Proverbs, Ecclesiastes.* AB 18. Doubleday, 1965. 2. Fox, M. *Proverbs 1–9.* AB 18A. Doubleday, 2000. 3. Whybray, R. N. *Proverbs.* NCB. Eerdmans, 1994.	1. Garret, D. A. *Proverbs, Ecclesiastes, Song of Songs.* NAC 14. Broadman and Holman, 1993. 2. Murphy, R. E. *Proverbs.* WBC 22. Word, 1999.	1. Kidner, D. *The Proverbs.* TOTC 15. Tyndale, 1964. 2. Hubbard, D. A. *Proverbs.* Mastering the Old Testament, Word, 1989.

BIBLICAL BOOK	SCHOLARLY COMMENTARIES		LAY COMMENTARIES
	NON-EVANGELICAL	EVANGELICAL	EVANGELICAL
Ecclesiastes	1. Scow, C. L. *Ecclesiastes*. AB 18C. Doubleday, 1997. 2. Fox, Michael. *Ecclesiastes*. Eerdmans, 1999. 3. Crenshaw, J. L. *Ecclesiastes: A Commentary*. OTL. Westminster, 1987. 4. Whybray, R. N. *Ecclesiastes*. NCB. Eerdmans, 1989.	1. Longman, T. *The Book of Ecclesiastes*. NICOT. Eerdmans, 1998. 2. Murphy, R. E. *Ecclesiastes*. WBC 23A. Word, 1992.	1. Eaton, M. *Ecclesiastes*. TOTC 16. InterVarsity, 1983. 2. Kaiser, W. C. *Ecclesiastes: Total Life*. Moody, 1979. 3. Hubbard, David A. *Ecclesiastes, Song of Solomon*. Mastering the Old Testament. Word, 1991.
Song of Solomon	1. Murphy, R. E. *Song of Songs*. HER. Fortress, 1990. 2. Pope, M. *Song of Songs*. AB 7. Doubleday, 1977. 3. Keel, Othmar. *The Song of Songs: A Continental Commentary*. Fortress, 1994.	1. Longman, T. *Song of Songs*. NICOT. Eerdmans, 2001. 2. Garrett, D. A. *Proverbs, Ecclesiastes, Song of Songs*. NAC 14. Broadman and Holman, 1993.	1. Carr, G. L. *Song of Songs*. TOTC 17. InterVarsity, 1984. 2. Provan, I. *Ecclesiastes, Song of Songs*. NIVAC. Zondervan, 2001.
Isaiah	1. Wildberger, H. *Isaiah 1–12; Isaiah 13–27; 28–39*. Fortress, 1997. 2. Blinkensopp, J. *Isaiah 1–39; Isaiah 40–55*. AB 19, 19A. Doubleday, 2000, 2002. 3. Baltzer, Klaus. *Deutero–Isaiah: A Commentary on Isaiah 40–55*. HER. Fortress, 2001. 4. Childs, B. S. *Isaiah*. OTL. Westminster John Knox, 2001.	1. Oswalt, J. N. *The Book of Isaiah Chapters 1–39; 40–66*. NICOT. Eerdmans, 1986, 1997. 2. Young, E. J. *The Book of Isaiah*. Eerdmans, 1972. 3. Motyer, J. A. *The Prophecy of Isaiah: An Introduction and Commentary*. InterVarsity, 1993.	1. Motyer, J. A. *Isaiah*. TOTC 18. InterVarsity, 1999. 2. Ridderbos, J. *Isaiah*. BSC. Zondervan, 1985.

BIBLICAL BOOK	SCHOLARLY COMMENTARIES		LAY COMMENTARIES
	NON-EVANGELICAL	EVANGELICAL	
Jeremiah	1. Holladay, W. *Jeremiah.* 2 Vols. HER. Fortress, 1986–89. 2. Bright, J. *Jeremiah.* AB 21. Doubleday, 1965.	1. Thompson, J. A. *The Book of Jeremiah.* NICOT. Eerdmans, 1980. 2. Huey, F. B. *Jeremiah, Lamentations.* NAC 16. Broadman and Holman, 1993.	1. Harrison, R. K. *Jeremiah and Lamentations.* TOTC 19. InterVarsity, 1973. 2. Kidner, D. *The Message of Jeremiah.* InterVarsity, 1987.
Lamentations	1. Hillers, D. R. *Lamentations.* AB 7A. Doubleday, 1972. 2. Gordis, R. *The Song of Songs and Lamentations.* KTAV, 1947.	1. Provan, I. *Lamentations.* NCB. Eerdmans, 1991. 2. Harrison, R. K. *Jeremiah and Lamentations.* TOTC 19. InterVarsity, 1973.	1. Kaiser, W. C. *A Biblical Approach to Personal Suffering.* Moody, 1982. 2. Ellison, H. L. "Lamentations." EBC. Zondervan, 1986 (6:695–733).
Ezekiel	1. Zimmerli, W. *Ezekiel 1–24; Ezekiel 25–48.* HER. 2 Vols. Fortress, 1979, 1983. 2. Greenberg, M. *Ezekiel 1–20; 21–37.* AB 22, 22A. Doubleday, 1983, 1997.	1. Block, D. I. *The Book of Ezekiel Chapters 1–24; Chapters 25–48.* NICOT. Eerdmans, 1997, 1998. 2. Allen, L. *Ezekiel 1–19; Ezekiel 20–48.* WBC 28, 29. Word, 1990, 1994.	1. Taylor, J. B. *Ezekiel.* TOTC 20. InterVarsity, 1969. 2. Alexander, R. H. "Ezekiel." EBC. Zondervan, 1986 (6:737–996)
Daniel	1. Collins, J. J. *Daniel.* HER. Fortress, 1993. 2. Hartmann, L., and A. DiLella. *The Book of Daniel.* AB 23. Doubleday, 1978.	1. Miller, Stephen R. *Daniel.* NAC 18. Broadman and Holman, 1994. 2. Goldingay, J. E. *Daniel.* WBC 30. Word, 1989.	1. Baldwin, J. G. *Daniel.* TOTC 21. InterVarsity, 1978. 2. Longman, T. *Daniel.* NIVAC. Zondervan, 1999.

	SCHOLARLY COMMENTARIES		LAY COMMENTARIES
BIBLICAL BOOK	**NON-EVANGELICAL**	**EVANGELICAL**	**EVANGELICAL**
Hosea	1. Wolff, H. W. *A Commentary on the Book of the Prophet Hosea.* HER. Fortress, 1974. 2. Anderson, F. I., and D. N. Freedman. *Hosea.* AB 24. Doubleday, 1980. 3. Mays, J. L. *Hosea: A Commentary.* OTL. Westminster, 1969.	1. Stuart, D. *Hosea–Jonah.* WBC 31. Word, 1987. 2. Hubbard, D. A. *Hosea.* TOTC 22. InterVarsity, 1989.	1. McComisky, T. E. "Hosea." *The Minor Prophets.* Baker, 1992–98. 2. Wood, L. J. "Hosea." EBC. Zondervan. 1985 (7:161–225).
Joel	1. Wolff, H. W. *A Commentary on the Book of the Prophet Hosea.* HER. Fortress, 1974. 2. Anderson, F. I., and D. N. Freedman. *Hosea.* AB 24. Doubleday, 1980. 3. Crenshaw, J. L. *Joel: New Translation with Introduction and Commentary.* AB 24C. Doubleday, 1995.	1. Stuart, D. *Hosea–Jonah.* WBC 31. Word, 1987. 2. Hubbard, D. A. *Joel and Amos.* TOTC 22B. InterVarsity, 1989.	1. Dillard, R. B. "Joel." *The Minor Prophets.* Baker, 1992–98. 2. Patterson, R. "Joel." EBC. Zondervan, 1985 (7:229–266).
Amos	1. Wolff, H. W. *A Commentary on the Books of the Prophets Joel and Amos.* HER. Fortress, 1977. 2. Paul, S. M. *Amos: A Commentary on the Book of Amos.* HER. Fortress, 1991. 3. Andersen, F. I., and D. N. Freedman. *Amos.* AB 24A. Doubleday, 1989. 4. Mays, J. L. *Amos: A Commentary.* OTL. Westminster, 1969.	1. Stuart, D. *Hosea–Jonah.* WBC 31. Word, 1987. 2. Hubbard, D. A. *Joel and Amos.* TOTC 22B. InterVarsity, 1989. 3. Smith, G. V. *Amos: A Commentary.* Zondervan, 1989.	1. McComiskey, T. E. "Amos." EBC. Zondervan, 1985 (7:269–331). 2. Motyer, J. A. *The Message of Amos: The Day of the Lion.* BST. InterVarsity, 1974.

(continued)

BIBLICAL BOOK	SCHOLARLY COMMENTARIES		LAY COMMENTARIES
	NON-EVANGELICAL	EVANGELICAL	EVANGELICAL
Obadiah	1. Wolff, H. W. *Obadiah and Jonah*. Augsburg, 1986. 2. Raabe, P. *Obadiah*. AB 24D. Doubleday, 1996.	1. Stuart, D. *Hosea–Jonah*. WBC 31. Word, 1987. 2. Allen, L. C. *The Books of Joel, Obadiah, Jonah, and Micah*. NICOT. Eerdmans, 1976.	1. Alexander, D., D. W. Baker, and B. Waltke. *Obadiah, Jonah, and Micah*. TOTC 23A. InterVarsity, 1988. 2. Niehaus, J. J. "Obadiah." *The Minor Prophets*. Baker, 1992–1998.
Jonah	1. Sasson, J. *Jonah*. AB 24B. Doubleday, 1990. 2. Wolff, H. W. *Obadiah and Jonah*. Augsburg, 1986. 3. Simon, U. *Jonah*. JPSC, 1999.	1. Stuart, D. *Hosea–Jonah*. WBC 31. Word, 1987. 2. Allen, L. C. *The Books of Joel, Obadiah, Jonah, and Micah*. NICOT. Eerdmans, 1976.	1. Alexander, D., D. W. Baker, and B. Waltke. *Obadiah, Jonah, and Micah*. TOTC 23A. InterVarsity, 1988.
Micah	1. Hillers, D. R. *Micah*. HER. Fortress, 1984. 2. Anderson, F. I., and D. N. Freedman. *Micah*. AB 24E. Doubleday, 2000. 3. Mays, J. L. *Micah*. Westminster, 1976. 4. Wolff, H. W. *Micah the Prophet*. Fortress, 1981.	1. Smith, R. L. *Micah–Malachi*. WBC 32. Word, 1984. 2. Allen, L. C. *The Books of Joel, Obadiah, Jonah, and Micah*. NICOT. Eerdmans, 1976.	1. Alexander, D., D. W. Baker, and B. Waltke. *Obadiah, Jonah, and Micah*. TOTC 23A. InterVarsity, 1988. 2. McComsky, T. E. "Micah." EBC. Zondervan, 1985 (7:395–445). 3. Waltke, B. K. "Micah." *The Minor Prophets*. Baker, 1992–1998.
Nahum	1. Roberts, J. J. M. *Nahum, Habakkuk, and Zephaniah*. OTL. Westminster/Fortress, 1991.	1. Robertson, O. P. *The Books of Nahum, Habakkuk, and Zephaniah*. NICOT. Eerdmans, 1990. 2. Smith, R. L. *Micah–Malachi*. WBC 32. Word, 1984.	1. Longman, T. "Nahum." *The Minor Prophets*. Baker, 1993. 2. Baker, D. W. *Nahum, Habakkuk, Zephaniah*. TOTC 23B. InterVarsity, 1988.

(continued)

| BIBLICAL BOOK | SCHOLARLY COMMENTARIES | | LAY COMMENTARIES |
	NON-EVANGELICAL	EVANGELICAL	EVANGELICAL
Habakkuk	1. Roberts, J. J. M. *Nahum, Habakkuk, and Zephaniah.* OTL. Westminster/Fortress, 1991.	1. Robertson, O. P. *The Books of Nahum, Habakkuk, and Zephaniah.* NICOT. Eerdmans, 1990. 2. Smith, R. L. *Micah–Malachi.* WBC 32. Word, 1984.	1. Baker, D. W. *Nahum, Habakkuk, Zephaniah.* TOTC 23B. InterVarsity, 1988. 2. Bruce, F. F. "Habakkuk." *The Minor Prophets.* Baker, 1992–1998.
Zephaniah	1. Wolff, H. W. *A Commentary on the Books of the Prophets Joel and Amos.* HER. Fortress, 1977. 2. Berlin, Adele. *Zephaniah.* AB 25A. Doubleday, 2001. 3. Roberts, J. J. M. *Nahum, Habakkuk, and Zephaniah.* OTL. Westminster/Fortress, 1991.	1. Robertson, O. P. *The Books of Nahum, Habakkuk, and Zephaniah.* NICOT. Eerdmans, 1990. 2. Smith, R. L. *Micah–Malachi.* WBC 32. Word, 1984.	1. Baker, D. W. *Nahum, Habakkuk, Zephaniah.* TOTC 23B. InterVarsity, 1988. 2. Patterson, R. D. *Nahum, Habakkuk, Zephaniah.* WEC. Moody, 1991. 3. Walker, L. L. "Zephaniah." EBC. Zondervan, 1985 (7:537–565).
Haggai	1. Meyers, C., and E. Meyers. *Haggai and Zechariah 1–8.* AB 25B. Doubleday, 1987. 2. Wolff, H. W. *Haggai.* Augsburg, 1988. 3. Redditt, P. L. *Haggai, Zechariah and Malachi.* NCB. Eerdmans, 1995.	1. Verheof, P. A. *The Books of Haggai and Malachi.* NICOT. Eerdmans, 1987. 2. Smith, R. L. *Micah–Malachi.* WBC 32. Word, 1984.	1. Baldwin, J. G. *Haggai, Zechariah, Malachi.* TOTC 24. InterVarsity, 1972. 2. Wiseman, D. J. "Haggai." NBC. Eerdmans, 1970.

(continued)

BIBLICAL BOOK	SCHOLARLY COMMENTARIES		LAY COMMENTARIES
	NON-EVANGELICAL	EVANGELICAL	EVANGELICAL
Zechariah	1. Meyers, C., and E. Meyers. *Haggai and Zechariah 1–8.* AB 25B. Doubleday, 1987. 2. Redditt, P. L. *Haggai, Zechariah and Malachi.* NCB. Eerdmans, 1995. 3. Peterson, D. L. *Haggai and Zechariah 1–8.* OTL. Westminster, 1984. 4. Peterson, D. L. *Zechariah 9–11 and Malachi.* OTL. Westminster John Knox, 1995.	1. Robertson, O. P. *The Books of Nahum, Habakkuk, and Zechariah.* NICOT. Eerdmans, 1990. 2. Smith, R. L. *Micah–Malachi.* WBC 32. Word, 1984.	1. Baldwin, J. G. *Haggai, Zechariah, Malachi.* TOTC 24. InterVarsity, 1972. 2. McComiskey, T. E. "Zechariah." *The Minor Prophets.* Baker, 1992–1998.
Malachi	1. Hill, A. E. *Malachi.* AB 25D. Doubleday, 1998. 2. Redditt, P. L. *Haggai, Zechariah and Malachi.* NCB. Eerdmans, 1995. 3. Peterson, D. L. *Zechariah 9–14 and Malachi.* OTL. Westminster John Knox, 1995.	1. Verheof, P. A. *The Books of Haggai and Malachi.* NICOT. Eerdmans, 1987. 2. Smith, R. L. *Micah–Malachi.* WBC 32. Word, 1984.	1. Baldwin, J. G. *Haggai, Zechariah, Malachi.* TOTC 24. InterVarsity, 1972. 2. Stuart, D. K. "Malachi." *The Minor Prophets.* Baker, 1992–1998. 3. Kaiser, W. C. *Malachi: God's Unchanging Love.* Baker, 1984.

OLD TESTAMENT
TEXTUAL CRITICISM
WORKSHEET

F ill out the following chart to determine the most plausible reading of an Old Testament text. Completing
this worksheet for a specific passage will ensure that
you are prepared to answer questions that arise about the
text, either during the sermon or afterward.

PASSAGE:_____

EVIDENCE FROM TEXTUAL TRADITION	EVIDENCE FROM MANUSCRIPTS OR VERSIONS
Codex Leningradensis (BHS): Translation:	Sources in agreement with MT:
Other MT Readings:	Other Readings:

EVALUATION	
Most Plausible MT Readings:	Other Plausible Readings:

Most Plausible Reading of the Text:
Reasons:

APPENDIX

C

HEBREW
WORD STUDY

An Old Testament Hebrew word study provides the foundation for any further study of a passage. It is crucial to know what individual words mean in order to understand a passage as a whole. Every Hebrew word has a range of meanings and several Hebrew words may overlap in meanings. It is the exegete's job to determine the specific range of meaning for each word and determine which nuance is most appropriate for a given passage. Hebrew word studies are most beneficial when they are thorough and exhaustive. Such a level of thoroughness can be obtained by using the following process.[*]

1. Determine the Frequency of the Hebrew Word. Note how often the Hebrew word occurs in the Old Testament and list any notable features about its frequency (e.g., Is it a common word? Does it appear to be a technical term? Does it occur in legal texts? Is it commonly found in ritual contexts?). Use a Hebrew concordance (one of the easiest to use is George V. Wigram, *The Englishman's Hebrew Concordance of Old Testament* [Peabody, MA: Hendrickson, 1996]) to obtain word frequencies and any collocations (i.e., words that are commonly used with it; a good source for those is Abraham Even-Shoshan, ed., *A New Concordance of the Old Testament*, 2nd ed. [Grand Rapids: Baker, 1989]). Are there any notable collocations? Is the word used in any special phrases? Is it used

---

[*] A special thanks to Dr. Dennis R. Magary for providing a significant foundation for further study in Hebrew words.

only in certain parts of Scripture? Does any book or author prefer this word or use it in a special way? Are there important observations about its distributions in the books in which it occurs? Historically when is the word first used? Is it a common word or does a synonym occur more frequently? If a word is used infrequently, then be very careful to record each occurrence and examine each context. Does the word occur more frequently in the Law and does it appear to have a very technical usage; or is it common in books of poetry and possess a more figurative meaning?

2. Record the Basic Lexical Meanings of the Word. Generally a lexicon will provide the basic meanings of Hebrew words. Use Koehler and Baumgartner (*HALOT*) or Brown, Driver, and Briggs (BDB) to determine these meanings. Note as many of the possible meanings and references as to where these meanings occur. Are there any specific passages that are crucial for determining the meaning of this word? Sometimes related words are mentioned or a root meaning from which other words may have developed. It may be helpful to examine older lexicons (e.g., BDB) and compare them to the newer ones (e.g., *HALOT*). Determine if there are any homonyms for your word (i.e., words which look like your word, but have a different meaning). If you are examining a noun, adjective, or adverb, check for any connections with verbs that appear similar. At this point be careful not to assume a connection between two words just because they look similar; nevertheless there may be legitimate connections. In poetic passages, carefully examine the parallel structure for any nuances or additional connotations of your word. Are there unusual usages of your word? Are there nonbiblical inscriptions that use this word? (Probably the best tool for determining this is the two-volume *Ancient Hebrew Inscriptions: Corpus and Concordance*, edited by G. I. Davies [Cambridge: University of Cambridge Press, 2004].) Also check for journal articles on this word—scholars may have made strides in delineating its meaning.

3. Examine the Septuagint (Greek) Equivalent(s) of the Hebrew Word. Use the index to Hatch and Redpath (i.e., Takamitsu Muraoka, *Hebrew/Aramaic Index to the Septuagint: Keyed to the Hatch-Redpath Concordance* [Grand Rapids: Baker, 1998]) to find any Greek equivalents.

Also note references so that they can be examined. You may need a Greek lexicon (e.g., BDAG) to determine the meaning of specific Greek words. How do the authors of the Septuagint render your Hebrew word? Do they seem to have understood what the Hebrew text was getting at? What is the range of meanings of the Greek words used to translate this Hebrew word and how well do they overlap in meaning? Be aware that these are two very different languages and that Greek equivalents may not correspond precisely to a Hebrew word.

4. Evaluate Lexical and/or Conceptual Synonyms. Are there any words similar in meaning to the word you are studying? Even-Shoshan's Hebrew concordance sometimes lists synonyms under the heading קרובים (i.e., "near words") and the *New International Dictionary of Old Testament Theology and Exegesis* (*NIDOTTE*), edited by Willem VanGemeren (Grand Rapids: Zondervan, 1997) may also provide synonyms. How are these similar words related to your word? Remember there may have been times when the authors of the Old Testament books had to choose your specific word over others which were similar, so determine the specific nuances of the word you are studying. Examine parallel passages containing synonyms to determine their range of meaning(s). Are there other Hebrew words translated with the same English word in various English translations? It may be helpful to develop a chart listing how the various English translations have rendered this word. What other words are conceptually related to your word (e.g., sin, transgression, iniquity, etc.)? Record these words with their basic lexical forms and meanings. The following chart can help determine how various synonyms differ and their specific nuances:

	נָבִיא	חֹזֶה	רֹאֶה	אִישׁ־אֱלֹהִים
Earliest/latest term				
Broadest/narrowest term				
Verbs commonly used with it				
Technical/common usage				
Theological Implications				
Special nuances of the word				

5. Research Any Significant Etymological Data. Is your word a fairly common Semitic word and/or are there any similarities to other Semitic words? Is there any traceable development in your word's meaning or formation? The best place to find this type of information is in *HALOT*. The etymological data found in BDB is generally out-of-date and of questionable value. Is your word part of any biblical or nonbiblical names? How is this word related to any Modern Hebrew words? However, a note of caution should be added here: often etymological data "preaches well," but may not be the author's intended meaning in a specific passage. For example, when people use the English expression "goodbye," the fact that the expression originates from "God be with you" is nowhere in the intended meaning.

6. Examine Any Theological Use of the Word. Some Hebrew words are used primarily in a theological context in the Old Testament and therefore it is important to note this usage. Examine each context to see how the word is used. A rather common concept can take on important theological implications in the Old Testament, such as "covenant," "sacrifice," or even "atonement."

7. Compare Modern English Translations. How do English translations render this word? Modern translations often provide the reader with an accurate and up-to-date interpretation of specific words. Select texts that are important to the meaning of your word and search through them thoroughly to determine if translators have consistently rendered a specific English word for that Hebrew word. One goal is to determine whether translators have provided an accurate translation of your word or if they missed a particular nuance or intended connotation. Have the English translators treated the word fairly in each passage or have they violated or obscured fine distinctions that should be maintained? Why do you think translational differences have occurred and are there rationales behind them? Identify which versions provide either important breakthroughs in translation or ones that poorly translate the intended meaning of your word.

8. Summarize Your Findings. If you have done careful and thorough research up to this point, then you should be able to formulate some accurate statements regarding a word's meaning, usage, and special significance. Take care to precisely formulate your conclusions about your specific word and do not overstate your conclusions. If the word is used primarily in specific contexts or under specific situations, note them. Why is this specific word used in a given context? What differentiates it from other similar words? What is the biblical author trying to convey by using this specific word? Since a word can have only one intended meaning in any given passage, note differences in meaning or specific meanings when used by particular Old Testament authors.

9. Prepare a Working Bibliography. List those works that were most important for determining the meaning of the word. Commonly used tools (e.g., BDB, *HALOT*, Even-Shoshan) need not be listed unless they provided significant information not found elsewhere. Instead, list lesser known works, such as journal articles, contributions in Festschriften, monographs, and notes in commentaries. Keeping track of helpful resources will enable you to recheck your conclusions should you have additional questions.

APPENDIX
D

SERMON WORKSHEET

Definition: An Old Testament Sermon Worksheet contains three parts: (1) an analysis of the passage indicating how its phrases are syntactically related to one another; (2) a basic sermon outline of the passage; and (3) a sentence that summarizes the key idea of the passage.*

I. Preparing a Syntactical Analysis
   A. The syntactical analysis is intended to give a visual layout of the structure of the passage and is a tool to help you think more clearly as to how the passage fits together. Highlight key words and make special grammatical and syntactical notes right on the syntactical analysis. It may be helpful to mark up the syntactical analysis with various colors or notations to aid in understanding the passage.
   B. A syntactical analysis can be made in either English or Hebrew, but Hebrew is preferable. Every English translation has to make grammatical/syntactical decisions as to the meaning of the text, often allowing for a variety of interpretations. Thus, going back to the original text is the only way to figure out which interpretation is the most likely.

---

* A special thanks to Dr. Walter C. Kaiser for providing a significant foundation for further study in the preparation of Old Testament sermons.

C. Read through the Old Testament passage to determine the natural divisions of the passage. At this point it is important to determine how much of the passage you will preach. Too much, and you will be constantly frustrated by trying to hurry through to cover all the material. Too little, and the congregation may be bored trying to get through the book. Chapters or psalms provide natural breaks, but be careful to avoid breaking up a unit of thought if it crosses over into another chapter.

D. Next, determine the natural divisions of the preaching passage. Divide the passage into paragraphs (prose) or strophes (poetry). These units will provide the basic sections of your syntactical outline and your sermon. Be careful not to assume that the verse divisions or paragraph divisions are correct. Leave a margin of two or three inches for writing a sermon or teaching outline on the right side (Hebrew) or left side (Greek, English) and draw a line to divide your syntactical outline from your sermon outline. (See the syntactical outlines in appendix E.)

E. Read through the paragraph or strophe several times to determine the key thought and the theme sentence (or line/unit in poetry) of the section. Put your theme sentence next to that line, but remember to leave room for the verse numbers.

F. Next, determine how each unit or phrase relates to the theme sentence of that paragraph or strophe. If the theme sentence does not appear at the beginning of the paragraph, place all the preceding clauses, phrases, or sentences in their appropriate indentation above the word or phrase that they modify with an arrow pointing *down* to that word. Then place the topic sentence out to the margin.

G. Examine how the clauses are related by linking words, such as "and," "but," "either or/neither nor," and "for" (this English word can also link subordinate causal clauses); then indicate the connection with these words to preceding clauses or succeeding ones.

H. Bracket all compound subjects, predicates, or objects after placing them on a separate line. However, single modifiers should be left on the same line as their clause.

I. Dependent clauses or a series of modifiers should be indented and subordinated under the words or phrases they modify in the topic sentence or main clause, with a vertical arrow *up* to those words. When dependent clauses or modifiers precede the independent clauses in the text, they should be indented above the word in the main clause it is related to with a vertical arrow pointing *down* to it.

J. The types of subordinate clauses may be indicated by the following abbreviations:

Con—Concessive (since)	A—Adversive (but)
Cond—Conditional (if)	Cir—Circumstantial (since, seeing that)
T—Temporal (when)	Rel—Relative (who, which, that)
P—Purpose (in order that, so)	L—Locative (in)
R—Result (so that)	I—Instrumental (by means of)
C—Causal (because)	

K. Parenthetical material may be enclosed in parentheses.

II. Preparing the Sermon Outline
Now study the syntactical analysis to see how the material is organized in each paragraph (or strophe) and how the parts of the biblical passage are related. This information can be put in the two- or three-inch margin on the right side (Hebrew) or left side (Greek, English).

A. Determine the central idea of each paragraph (or strophe) and the timeless principle that may be developed from it. The central ideas of the paragraphs (or strophes) will become the main points of the sermon outline and they will be written in the margin. It is best not to use proper names (except God's name) or place names in order to be as applicable as possible. Work on these main points until they convey the biblical concepts of your passage in a meaningful way to those who will be listening to them.

B. Once you have determined the key principles of each paragraph (or strophe), find a key word that can tie them together. A key word is an abstract plural noun such as *lessons, reasons, truths,* or *areas* that reflects the author's purpose for the section. Once you have determined a key word that relates to each of the main points, you may have to work with each main point to make sure they are parallel to each other.

C. Check to make sure the points in your sermon reflect the grammatical structure of the biblical text as recorded on the right (or left).

D. Next, you can add subpoints beneath the main points, but make sure they follow the grammatical layout. Avoid making too many subpoints or including too much detail.

E. This outline is the basis of your proclamation of God's Word. Consider what God is trying to say to you and to your congregation through this passage.

III. Preparing the Summary Sentence

Developing a summary sentence will ensure that you know the key thought you intend to bring across to your listeners. From this you will develop clear and specific points of application that will meet the needs of those in your congregation.

A. *Determining the Central Point.* What is the crucial idea upon which all else hinges? What is the central point that illuminates the inner structure of this text? Formulate this point in a word or phrase. Better still—point to that key word or phrase in *the passage itself.*

B. *Developing the Summary Sentence.* Summarize the passage into one concluding summary sentence that states exactly what the passage is saying. It should be concise in words, but full of meaning to capture the totality of what is being said. If you cannot summarize it in one sentence, then you probably need to narrow down the main idea of the sermon more.

C. *How to Apply this Central Idea.* Determine the most important contemporary practical application from the universal principles developed in the sermon. Determine the best way to present this application through your sermon. Often people have difficulty appropriately applying biblical texts to their own situations without help. Think of as many practical ways as possible that the central idea can apply to the lives of the people in your congregation, but use only the best ones in your sermon.

APPENDIX
E

SYNTACTICAL
ANALYSIS OF
PSALM 23

W hat follows is two diagrams: an English syntactical
analysis of Psalm 23 and a Hebrew syntactical analysis of the same passage. The following symbols are
used to delineate the syntax:

Ⓒ = Causal

(Con) = Construct

Ⓘ = Instrumental

Ⓛ = Locative

Ⓣ = Temporal

Ⓡ = Results

The arrows in the following diagrams indicate how
phrases relate to each other. Phrases often relate to the
subject or verb of the previous phrase.

Whom Do You Trust?

Transitional Statement:
Psalm 23 contains three REASONS
why I can trust my God.

I. He is my Provider (vv. 1-3)

A. He supplies my needs (v. 1)

B. He provides bountifully (v. 2a)

C. He provides my emotional welfare (v. 2b)

D. He supplies spiritual wellness

1. Inner restoration (v. 3a)

2. Spiritual direction (v. 3b)

¹The LORD is my shepherd
(R) I shall not lack.

²He makes me lie down [in green pastures;]
(L)
He leads me [beside quiet waters.]
(L)
³He restores my soul;
(L)
He guides me [in the paths (of righteousness)]
(C) for His name's sake.

II. He Is My Protector (vv. 4–5)

Protection amidst my greatest fears

A. Death (v. 4)

B. Enemies (v. 5a)

C. Lack of provisions (v. 5b)

III. He Is My Promise (v. 6)

A. God's blessings during life (v. 6a)

B. God's fellowship during life (v. 6b)

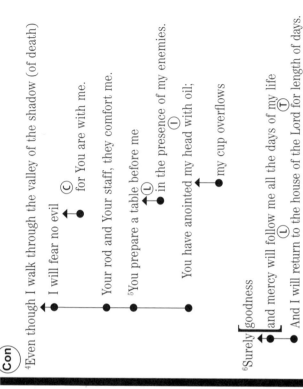

(Con)

⁴Even though I walk through the valley of the shadow (of death)

I will fear no evil

Ⓒ for You are with me.

Your rod and Your staff, they comfort me.

⁵You prepare a table before me

Ⓛ in the presence of my enemies.

You have anointed my head with oil;

Ⓘ my cup overflows

⁶Surely goodness

Ⓛ and mercy will follow me all the days of my life

Ⓣ

And I will return to the house of the Lord for length of days.

Summary Statement: I can trust God to provide for me (His sheep) as a loving shepherd provides for his sheep.

Whom Do You Trust?

Transitional Statement: three
REASONS why I can trust my God.

I. He is my Provider (vv. 1-3)

A. He supplies my needs (v. 1)

B. He provides bountifully (v. 2a)

C. He provides my emotional welfare (v. 2b)

D. He supplies spiritual wellness

1. Inner restoration (v. 3a)

2. Spiritual direction (v. 3b)

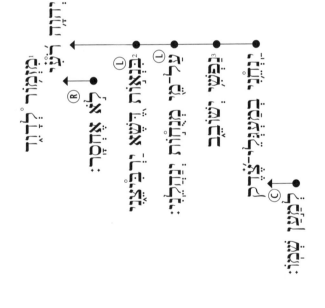

II. He Is My Protector (vv. 4–5)

Protection amidst my greatest fears

A. Death (v. 4)

B. Enemies (v. 5a)

C. Lack of provisions (v. 5b)

III. He Is My Promise (v. 6)

A. God's blessings during life (v. 6a)

B. God's fellowship during life (v. 6b)

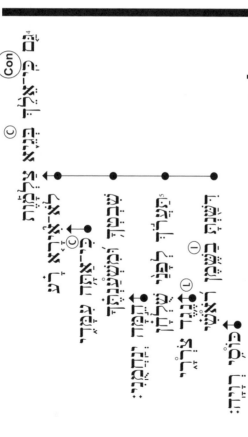

Summary Statement: I can trust God to provide for me (His sheep) as a loving shepherd provides for his sheep.

AUTHOR INDEX

SCRIPTURE INDEX

BIBLE
PERMISSIONS

Kregel Academic & Professional

Hebrew

and **Old**

Testament

Resources

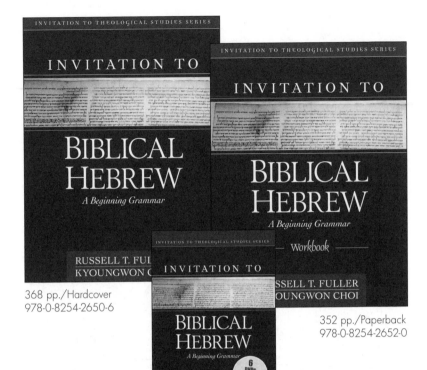

INVITATION TO THEOLOGICAL STUDIES SERIES

INVITATION TO

BIBLICAL HEBREW
A Beginning Grammar

RUSSELL T. FULLER
KYOUNGWON CHOI

368 pp./Hardcover
978-0-8254-2650-6

INVITATION TO THEOLOGICAL STUDIES SERIES

INVITATION TO

BIBLICAL HEBREW
A Beginning Grammar
Workbook

RUSSELL T. FULLER
KYOUNGWON CHOI

352 pp./Paperback
978-0-8254-2652-0

INVITATION TO THEOLOGICAL STUDIES SERIES

INVITATION TO

BIBLICAL HEBREW
A Beginning Grammar

6 DVDs
38 Lectures

RUSSELL T. FULLER
KYOUNGWON CHOI

38 lectures/6 DVDs
978-0-8254-2651-3

Based on years of success in the classroom, *Invitation to Biblical Hebrew* provides an ideal textbook in three components for the beginning Hebrew student.

Clear, accurate, and pedagogically sound, the textbook focuses on the basics of phonology (sounds) and morphology (forms) so that the student is able to learn the language by reason and rule rather than rote memorization. The supplemental workbook provides the student with additional drills, quizzes, and reviews not found in the textbook. An answer key is also provided.

The six DVD set features thirty-eight lectures by Dr. Fuller, corresponding to each lesson of the textbook. Each session explains, illustrates, and reinforces the principles and rules covered in the text through oral and visual presentations. These pedagogically innovative DVDs enable students to come to class better prepared, and can be viewed at home when a student misses a class or needs additional instruction.

COMMENDATION FROM THE CLASSROOM

"I have used *Invitation to Biblical Hebrew* in teaching Hebrew I–II to seminary students for five years. After switching to this method of teaching, my students' retention of Hebrew knowledge increased dramatically. I have my students read the chapter, watch the video over the chapter, and then do the questions at the end of the chapter—all before class. I then review the material in class and the students complete drills. After class, students do the chapter exercises and translation to turn in for the following class. The use of the videos alone increases comprehension and reduces the number of questions students have in class. Also, if a student is absent or just did not understand a given lesson, it is easy for them to get back on track with the video lectures. I wholeheartedly endorse Fuller and Choi's *Invitation to Biblical Hebrew*. It has worked well for me and for my students."

—Eric A. Mitchell
Assistant Professor of Biblical Backgrounds and Archaeology
Southwestern Baptist Theological Seminary

AUTHORS

Russell T. Fuller (Ph.D., Hebrew Union College) is associate professor of Old Testament interpretation at The Southern Baptist Theological Seminary in Louisville, Kentucky.

Kyoungwon Choi (Ph.D., The Southern Baptist Theological Seminary) is assistant professor of Old Testament and Hebrew at Temple Baptist Seminary.

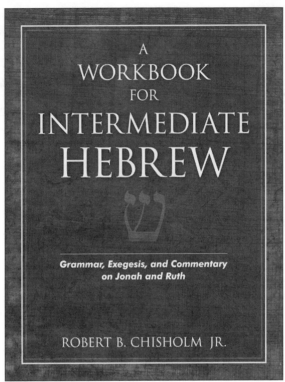

A
WORKBOOK
FOR
INTERMEDIATE
HEBREW

*Grammar, Exegesis, and Commentary
on Jonah and Ruth*

ROBERT B. CHISHOLM JR.

320 pp./Paperback
978-0-8254-2390-1

Designed as a bridge between elementary and intermediate biblical Hebrew, this workbook encourages the student to engage the text and reinforces patterns and principles of Hebrew grammar and syntax. The student is expertly guided by well-crafted questions related to morphology and syntax, and asked to provide a rough translation and to outline the structure of Jonah and Ruth. Answers to all questions are provided, which gives students instant feedback.

A Workbook for Intermediate Hebrew can be easily used in conjunction with most Hebrew grammars. References to grammars by Pratico/Van Pelt and Fuller/Choi are included in the text itself; additional grammars, commentaries, lexicons, and other reference works are mentioned in the footnotes. Other features include both a useful parsing guide (presented in eleven charts) and glossaries for Jonah and Ruth. Each glossary is keyed to both BDB and HALOT so students can easily access a more thorough discussion of any given word.

PRAISE FOR *A WORKBOOK FOR INTERMEDIATE HEBREW*

"After studying the Hebrew text of Jonah and Ruth with the aid of this workbook, students will be much further down the path of being competent readers and interpreters of the Hebrew Bible."

—Mark D. Futato
Reformed Theological Seminary
Author, *Beginning Biblical Hebrew*

"A much-needed tool for the study of morphology, grammar, and syntax in biblical exegesis, this workbook is a welcome addition for teaching intermediate Hebrew. It is also a great resource for any who wish to review Hebrew grammar and syntax on their own as they study the texts of Jonah and Ruth."

—Allen P. Ross
Beeson Divinity School
Author, *Introducing Biblical Hebrew*

"With a nice balance between assignments and comments about forms and structure, this workbook guides the student step-by-step. The student who completes the exercises will be better equipped to confront a Hebrew text and interpret it properly."

—Thomas J. Finley
Talbot School of Theology
Coauthor, *How Biblical Languages Work*

"This interactive workbook is a fantastic tool provided by a longtime teacher of Hebrew who knows what needs to be done, knows how to do it, and does it in an interesting way."

—Richard E. Averbeck
Trinity Evangelical Divinity School

AUTHOR

Robert B. Chisholm Jr. (Th.D., Dallas Theological Seminary) is chair of the Old Testament department and professor of Old Testament studies at Dallas Theological Seminary. A veteran teacher of Hebrew, he is the author of several books, including *From Exegesis to Exposition: A Practical Guide to Using Biblical Hebrew*.

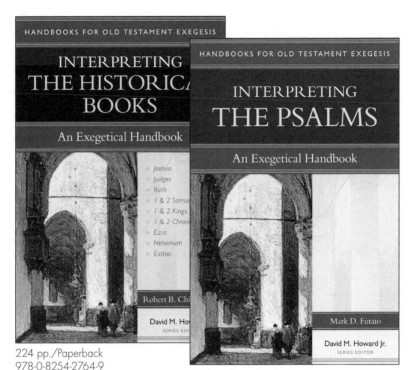

HANDBOOKS FOR OLD TESTAMENT EXEGESIS

INTERPRETING
THE HISTORICAL
BOOKS

An Exegetical Handbook

⬦ Joshua
⬦ Judges
⬦ Ruth
⬦ 1 & 2 Samuel
⬦ 1 & 2 Kings
⬦ 1 & 2 Chronicles
⬦ Ezra
⬦ Nehemiah
⬦ Esther

Robert B. Chisholm

David M. Howard Jr.
SERIES EDITOR

HANDBOOKS FOR OLD TESTAMENT EXEGESIS

INTERPRETING
THE PSALMS

An Exegetical Handbook

Mark D. Futato

David M. Howard Jr.
SERIES EDITOR

224 pp./Paperback
978-0-8254-2764-9

272 pp./Paperback
978-0-8254-2765-7

The Old Testament displays a remarkable literary and theological unity through a variety of genres. But applying a single, one-size-fits-all method of exegesis can lead to confusion, misunderstanding, and even wrong interpretations or applications. Careful attention to differences in genre is, then, a critical component of exegesis.

The Handbooks for Old Testament Exegesis series (HOTE) provides readers with an enhanced understanding of different Old Testament genres and strategies for interpretation. The volumes are written by seasoned scholar-teachers who possess extensive knowledge of their disciplines and lucid writing abilities. Primarily intended to serve as textbooks for graduate-level exegesis courses, HOTE volumes (1) introduce genre(s); (2) consider the major themes in individual books and canonical sections; (3) discuss such diverse matters as historical and culture backgrounds, critical questions, and textual matters; (4) provide guidelines of exegesis and strategies for proclaiming each text. All volumes include a glossary of technical terms.

PRAISE FOR INTERPRETING THE HISTORICAL BOOKS

"Chisholm's presentation of the nature of narrative in literature, of the purpose of each narrative book, and of the interpretive methods to be used is judicious, balanced, and circumspect at every turn. Every seminary student needs to learn what this book teaches."

—**John H. Walton**
Wheaton College and Graduate School

AVAILABLE AND FORTHCOMING VOLUMES

Interpreting the Pentateuch
Forthcoming
Peter T. Vogt (Bethel Seminary)

Interpreting the Historical Books
Available
Robert B. Chisholm Jr. (Dallas Theological Seminary)

Interpreting the Wisdom Literature
Forthcoming
Richard L. Schultz (Wheaton College and Graduate School)

Interpreting the Psalms
Available
Mark D. Futato (Reformed Theological Seminary)

Interpreting the Prophets
Forthcoming
Michael A. Grisanti (The Master's Seminary)

Interpreting Apocalyptic Literature
Forthcoming
Richard A. Taylor (Dallas Theological Seminary)

AUTHORS AND EDITOR

Robert B. Chisholm Jr. (Th.D., Dallas Theological Seminary) is the chair of the Old Testament department and professor of Old Testament studies at Dallas Theological Seminary. His books include *Handbook on the Prophets* and *From Exegesis to Exposition: A Practical Guide to Using Biblical Hebrew.*

Mark D. Futato (Ph.D., Catholic University of America) is Robert L. Maclellan Professor of Old Testament and academic dean at Reformed Theological Seminary in Orlando, Florida. He is the author of five books, including *Beginning Biblical Hebrew.*

David M. Howard Jr. (Ph.D., University of Michigan) is dean of the Center for Biblical and Theological Foundations, and professor of Old Testament at Bethel Seminary.

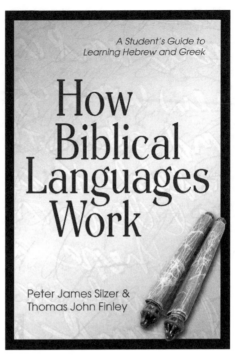

A Student's Guide to
Learning Hebrew and Greek

How
Biblical
Languages
Work

Peter James Silzer &
Thomas John Finley

256 pp./Paperback
978-0-8254-2644-5

This practical guide makes learning the biblical languages a less daunting task. By introducing students to characteristics and functions of all human language, experienced linguists Silzer and Finley create the basis from which to describe the major features of Hebrew and Greek: how sounds are pronounced, how words are put together, how phrases and clauses are structured, how words convey meaning, and how languages change. The book includes practical exercises, a glossary of linguistic and grammatical terms widely used in standard grammars of Greek and Hebrew, and other resources for further study.

"This marvelously clear and cogent introduction to biblical linguistics should be required reading for every student of Hebrew and Greek."

—**Mark L. Strauss**
Bethel Seminary, San Diego

GIVING
the SENSE

UNDERSTANDING AND USING OLD TESTAMENT HISTORICAL TEXTS

DAVID M. HOWARD JR.
MICHAEL A. GRISANTI
editors

482 pp./Paperback
978-0-8254-2892-0

Brimming with insights, this collection of essays covers the four major periods of Israel's history and explores the theological, literary, historical, and archaeological dimensions of each era. Some of the contributors include Robert B. Chisholm Jr., Eugene Merrill, Richard E. Averbeck, Allen P. Ross, Daniel I. Block, and Walter C. Kaiser Jr.

"Whether one's interests lean toward larger general issues or more focused technical questions, one will find much to like and learn in this very welcome collection."

—**V. Phillips Long**
Regent College, Vancouver